CUPS & CANS & PAPER PLATE FANS

CRAFT PROJECTS FROM RECYCLED MATERIALS

Phyllis Fiarotta & Noel Fiarotta

 Sterling Publishing Co., Inc.   New York

Color photos by Ray Solowinski
with assistance from Kelly Curtis

Edited by Jeanette Green

Library of Congress Cataloging-in-Publication Data

Fiarotta, Phyllis.
    Cups & cans & paper plate fans : craft projects from recycled
materials / by Phyllis Fiarotta and Noel Fiarotta.
        p.   cm.
    Includes index.
    Summary: Gives step-by-step instructions for making a variety of
craft projects from such recyclable items as paper bags, boxes,
cans, dairy containers, and jars.
    ISBN 0-8069-8528-3 :
    1. Handicraft—Juvenile literature.   2. Recycling (Waste, etc.)—
Juvenile literature.   [1. Handicraft.   2. Recycling (Waste)]
I. Fiarotta, Noel.   II. Title.   III. Title: Cups and cans and paper
plate fans.
TT160.F474   1992
745.58′4—dc20
                                                    91-41825
                                                         CIP
                                                          AC

10 9 8 7 6 5 4 3 2 1

First paperback edition published in 1993 by
Sterling Publishing Company, Inc.
387 Park Avenue South, New York, N.Y. 10016
© 1992 by Phyllis Fiarotta & Noel Fiarotta
Distributed in Canada by Sterling Publishing
% Canadian Manda Group, P.O. Box 920, Station U
Toronto, Ontario, Canada M8Z 5P9
Distributed in Great Britain and Europe by Cassell PLC
Villiers House, 41/47 Strand, London WC2N 5JE, England
Distributed in Australia by Capricorn Link Ltd.
P.O. Box 665, Lane Cove, NSW 2066
Manufactured in the United States of America
All rights reserved

Sterling ISBN 0-8069-8528-3 Trade
            0-8069-8529-1 Paper

This book is printed on recycled paper.

We dedicate this book to the memory of our parents whose overflowing love, generosity, and sense of humor still enriches our lives and enraptures our souls.

Contents

Recycling and You

The earth gives us many wonderful gifts to enjoy—like water to sail our boats on, forests to pitch our tents in, and playful breezes to send our kites soaring to the clouds. The earth also gives us the materials to build our sailing boats, pitch our cozy tents, and make our soaring kites. But there may be a problem in the future. We are using up the earth's materials, and most of them cannot be replaced. Some of these precious materials are *petroleum* for making plastic bottles, *aluminum* for soft drink cans, and *trees* for paper bags to hold our groceries.

But what happens to the bottles, cans, and bags after they are no longer needed? Many communities collect these disposable items so that they can be used again. This is called *recycling*. It is everyone's job to recycle. What can you do to recycle the things in your home that are headed for the trash? *Cups & Cans & Paper Plate Fans* is a book that will show you dozens of ways to turn ordinary nothings into extraordinary somethings. All it takes are these throwaways, art supplies, and lots of imagination.

Remember, it is always best for the environment to use a paper cup instead of a foam cup, a paper plate instead of a plastic plate, and paper bags instead plastic bags. And it is even better to use china or glass cups and plates that you do not have to throw away. But until these paper, foam, and plastic products are no longer a part of our everyday lives, this book will show you how to recycle them creatively.

Kitchen Craft Supplies

Dairy Containers

Dairy containers have many shapes, some with straight sides, some with slanted sides. Most are made of plastic, but there are also round cardboard tubs like the kind whipped margarine or butter comes in.

Some examples are sour cream (a), ricotta (b), ice cream (c), snack foods (d), whipped butter (e), cottage cheese (f), yogurt (g), cookies (h), party dip (i), margarine (j), whipped cream cheese (k), and deli salads (l).

Most are round like those below, but some are square with round sides.

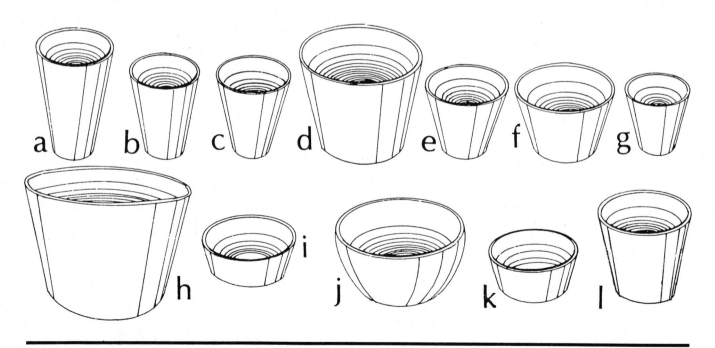

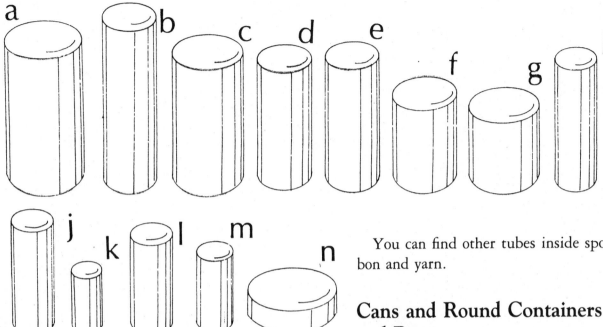

Jars and Bottles

Most jars are made of glass, but there are some plastic ones. Jars come in all sizes. Most are round.

Plastic bottles come in all sizes, colors, and shapes. Some have handles.

Tubes

Kitchen paper towels are rolled on a long cardboard tube. Bathroom tissues are rolled on a short tube.

You can find other tubes inside spools of ribbon and yarn.

Cans and Round Containers and Boxes

Tin cans are made in many sizes. Fruit juices come in large cans and tomato paste comes in small cans. A coffee tin has a removable plastic lid. Soft drink cans are made of aluminum.

There are also many round throwaways made of cardboard. Some examples of round containers are oatmeal (a), stacked potato chips (b), salt (c), bread crumbs (d), grated cheese (e), frosting (f), powdered fruit drink (g), dried herbs (h), cleanser (i), potato sticks (j), table salt and pepper (k), frozen juice (l), flavor enhancer (m), and cheese wedges (n).

Boxes

Boxes come in over a hundred sizes and shapes. They can be square, flat, long, big, and tiny.

Some examples of box shapes and sizes are flat—margarine sticks (a), large with equal sides—saltine crackers (b), standard—cookies and cereal (c), small and flat—candy (d), small and deep—tea (e), long and flat—spaghetti (f), small rectangle with equal sides—toothpaste (g), and large square—facial tissues (h).

Paper

Colored construction paper comes in packages of small-size sheets. Larger sheets are sold in art stores. For some projects, you may choose to use newspaper instead. Magazines, junk mail, and the comics will add some color and pattern to your project.

Poster boards are large sheets of lightweight cardboard made in many colors and sold by dime stores, stationery shops, or art suppliers.

Use food boxes for lightweight cardboard.

Use corrugated cartons or boxes for heavy cardboard.

Large brown paper grocery or shopping bags and brown wrapping paper yield large sheets of brown paper. Thin paper also comes with some dry cleaning.

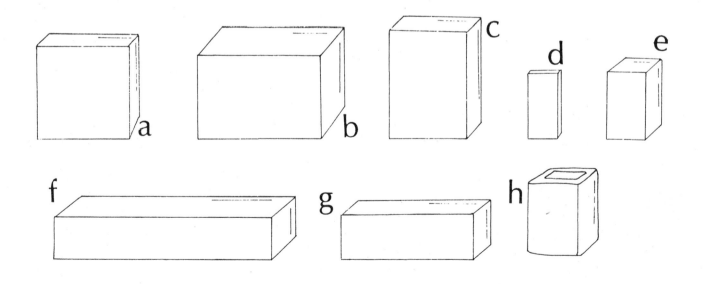

Peaked Cartons

Milk, fruit juice, and punch come in peaked cartons. The dairy carton
has four sides that are
equal in size. The top of
the dairy or other food
container is folded into
a peak.

The sizes are half gal-
lon (2 l.), quart (1 l.),
pint (half quart; 480
ml.), half pint (240
ml.), and quarter pint
(120 ml.).

Cups and Plates and Bags

Cups, plates, and bags or sacks are great kitchen
craft supplies.

Cups are made in hard and soft plastic, foam,
and paper. The most common sizes are the
3-ounce (90 ml.) bathroom cup, the 5-ounce
(150 ml.) kitchen cup, and the 8-ounce (240
ml.) regular cup.

Plates with plain colors are best for craft
projects. Plates are made of plastic, foam, paper,
and cardboard.

Bags made of plastic or paper range from sandwich size to grocery size.

Other Recyclables

Many things made of paper, plastic, metal, or
glass that are usually headed for the trash can or
dustbin may be a kitchen craft supply. There are
many throwaways you can use in craft projects
other than those in this book, like berry baskets
and the plastic rings that hold a six-pack of soft
drinks together.

Other Supplies

Crayons or felt-tip markers in various colors, a
paintbrush, and scissors come in handy. A sharpened pencil or a paper punch is useful for making
small holes. Cord is stronger than string; so cord
is best for hanging. Yarn (knitting wool) adds
fuzzy decoration, and it can be used to hang light
objects.

Transparent tape looks best when the tape
might show. But almost any kind of tape will
work nicely. Paste or white glue will stick to
paper, glass, plastic, or metal. White glue, unlike many other glues, is safe to use.

BAGS

Totem Pole

Totem poles are tall wood carvings once made by Native Americans of northwestern North America. They consist of many totems, one on top of the other, like the stories of an apartment building.

Totems are the symbols for tribes, clans, and families. Some of the familiar totem symbols are fish, birds, animals, plants, and other natural things. Bag a bunch of totems and stack them to the ceiling. Start with the owl, raccoon, and bear.

THE OWL

1. Place a bag on a table with the open end at the bottom.
2. Cut out the owl's eyes and beak from colored paper.
3. Paste the eyes and beak to the top half of the paper bag—on the side without printing (a). Draw on feathers and other details.
4. Open the bag and keep the open side facing up (b).
5. Cut halfway into the bag along the four sides (see arrows in drawing b).

THINGS YOU NEED
large brown paper grocery bags
colored paper ★ scissors ★ paste
crayons or markers ★ newspaper ★ tape

6. Cut newspaper into narrow strips (c).
7. Fill the bag up halfway with crumpled newspaper strips.
8. Fold over two opposite sides at the top of the bag (d). Fold over the other sides (e). Tape them in place.
9. Cut wings from colored paper. Tape them to the back of the bag (f).

THE RACCOON AND BEAR

1. Make the raccoon and bear in the same way you did the owl. Paste paper ears on both.
2. Stack the totem animals on top of each other.

a

b

c

d

e

f

Glowworm

Glowworms are tiny worms that will grow up to be fireflies. When it is dark, they glow as if they had tiny flashlights (torches) in their stomachs.

This glowworm is a friendly pal that reveals its smile when its switch is turned on. Keep it by your bed at night. If you should ever be afraid of the dark, this glowworm will brighten up a scary night.

THINGS YOU NEED
brown paper lunch bag ★ crayons or markers cord ★ flashlight (torch)

THE GLOWWORM

1. Place the bag on a table with the open end at the bottom.
2. Draw a face near the top of the bag with crayons or markers (a).
3. Place the head of a flashlight into the bag (b).
4. Gather the bag around the flashlight (c).
5. Tie the bag tightly to the flashlight with cord (c).
6. Turn on the flashlight to see the glowworm glow.

Character Masks

"Who's behind the mask?" your friends will ask. Masks are fun because they let you pretend you are somebody else or something else. You can be a ferocious animal, a friendly clown, or a frightening creature from outer space. Make a whole cast of characters and be a different *you* every day of the week.

THINGS YOU NEED
brown paper lunch bags
crayons or markers ★ scissors ★ paste
colored paper ★ pencil ★ cord or ribbon

THE MASK

1. Place a bag on a table with the open end at the bottom.
2. Draw eyes with crayons or markers. They should be where your eyes will be (a). Draw a nose and a mouth.
3. Cut out the eyes.
4. Cut out strips for the hair from colored paper. Cut slits into the strips (b).
5. Glue the hair to the top of the bag (c). You can also cut out and glue on eyelashes and a moustache.
6. Cut away the back of the bag (d).
7. Poke a hole into the center of each side of the bag with a pencil (e).
8. Tie the cord or ribbon into each hole (f).
9. Place the mask on your face and tie it in place.

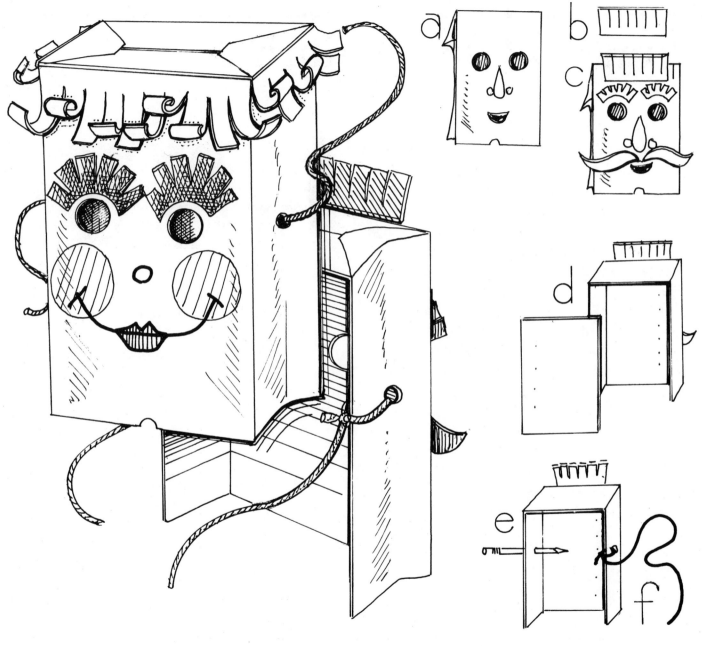

Stained-Glass Painting

Stained-glass windows are paintings in glass. They are made from many different pieces of colored glass held together by leading. When the sun shines through them, a wonderland of bright colors comes to life. Such windows can be seen in some churches, synagogues, mosques, houses, and fancy places. There may even be one in your home.

Create brilliant stained-glass paintings. All you need is a drawing, a sandwich bag, and the secret ingredient, salad oil. Hold your creation up to a light, or tape it to a window to see it shine brightly.

THINGS YOU NEED
plastic sandwich bag ★ sheet of typing paper scissors ★ black and colored markers salad oil ★ paper cup ★ cotton ball

6. Slip the drawing into the bag.
7. Tape the bag to a window.

THE STAINED GLASS

1. Cut paper to fit inside a plastic bag.
2. Draw a design on the paper with a black marker (a). Make the lines thick.
3. Color in the design with markers of different colors (b).
4. Pour a little salad oil into a paper cup.
5. Rub oil over the entire drawing with a cotton ball (c).

Bag of Flowers

When we give flowers as gifts, we usually present them in flowerpots or wrap them in colorful paper. If you want to say "I love you" or "I think you're pretty nice," here's how. Give a bouquet of flowers in a bag. There are many colorful silk, plastic, or dried flowers. Make a nice arrangement, place them in a sandwich bag, and add a pretty bow.

THINGS YOU NEED
brown paper lunch bag ★ ribbon
dried, plastic, or silk flowers

THE BAG

1. Open the bag and roll over a little of the top.
2. Tie a ribbon into a bow around the middle of the bag.
3. Add dried, plastic, or silk flowers to the bag.

CANS

Elephant Pencil Holder

There is a popular saying, "An elephant never forgets." Maybe that's because they have very little to remember.

Have you ever forgotten to bring a pencil to school? Have you ever looked for a pencil but couldn't find one? With this elephant's help, you will always remember where your pencils are.

THINGS YOU NEED
large can ★ large brown paper grocery bag paste ★ scissors ★ tape ★ crayons or markers brown or grey construction paper

THE PENCIL HOLDER

1. Ask an adult to remove the opened end of the large can. Wash the can.
2. From the grocery bag, cut out a piece of paper as tall as the can and long enough to wrap around it (a).
3. Wrap the paper around the can. Tape the paper in place (b).
4. Draw eyes and a triangle mouth on the front of the can (c).
5. From brown construction paper, cut a long trunk (d) and ears (e).
6. Paste the ears near the top of the can (f).
7. Curl the end of the trunk (g).
8. Paste the trunk to the can above the mouth.

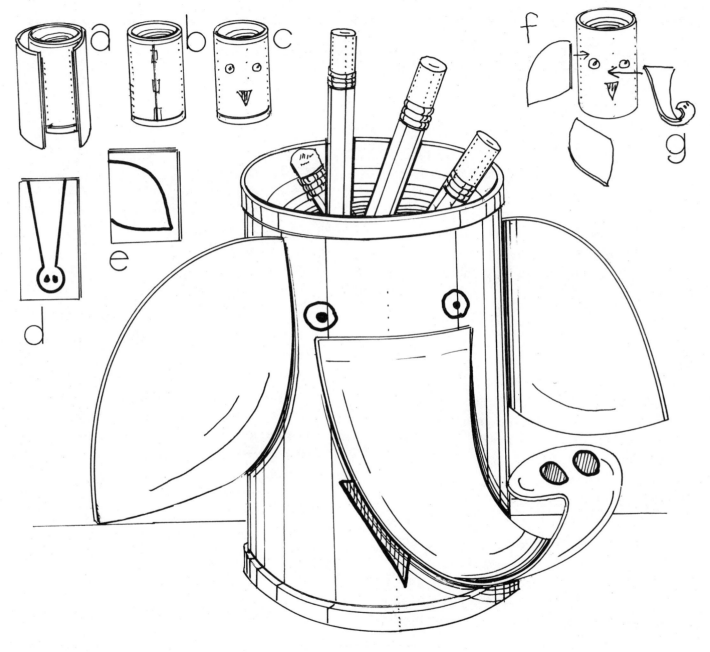

Life-Size Palm Tree

Palm trees are found in tropical places where the weather is hot. They are very tall, and you have to climb up really high to pick the coconuts.

Turn your room into a tropical island with one or more of these life-size palm trees. When the weather is cold outside, lie on your bed, close your eyes, and pretend you are on a beach in the Caribbean Sea.

THE PALM TREE

1. Ask an adult to remove one end of a large can. Place a large rock inside the can (a).
2. Tape the cans together to form the trunk of the tree (b). The can with the rock is at the bottom.
3. From a brown grocery bag, cut paper half the height of the can and long enough to wrap around it. Cut two for each can.
4. Cut slits into one long side of each paper to form a fringe (c).
5. Wrap a paper around the top can and tape it in place (d). The fringe should be at the top. Bend the fringe away from the can slightly.

THINGS YOU NEED
four to six large tin cans the same size
large rock ★ strong tape ★ scissors ★ paste
large brown paper grocery bags
two sheets of green poster board

6. Wrap another paper around the can as you did the first (e). It should overlap the first a little.
7. Continue wrapping and taping papers. Cover the entire trunk of the palm tree.
8. Cut each sheet of green poster board into three sections.
9. Draw a large leaf on each section (f). Cut them out.
10. Cut notches into both sides of each leaf (g).
11. Draw a vein design on each leaf (h).
12. Tape the leaves, one at a time, to the top of the trunk.

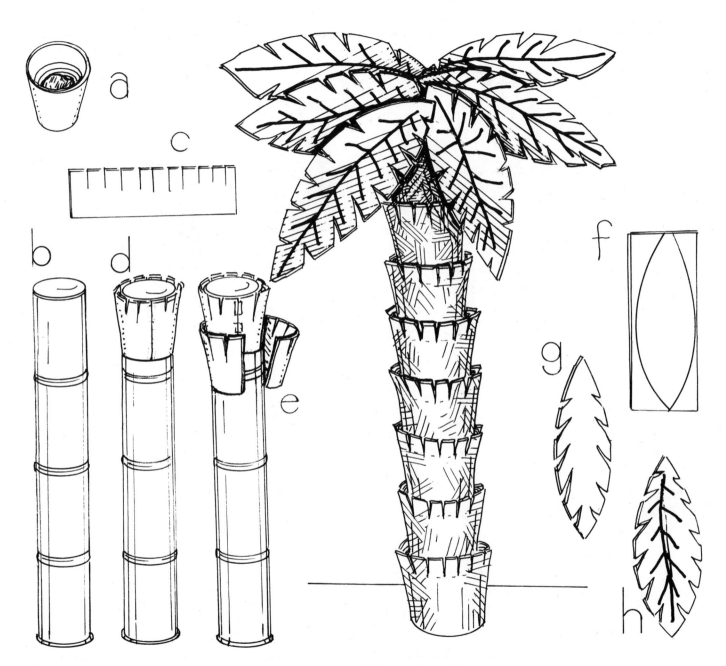

a

c

b   d   e

f

g

h

27

Bird Feeder

The blue jay, the chickadee, the kookaburra, and the robin are just a few of the wild birds you may see in your neighborhood. Unlike parakeets and canaries, which live in cages, wild birds make their homes in trees and bushes.

You can make sure they stay around by giving them birdseed every day. Hang this bird feeder outside your window or in a tree. Be sure not to give them too much food. They also have to eat other natural goodies.

THINGS YOU NEED
large can ★ cord ★ real or artificial ivy ★ tape colored paper ★ scissors ★ pencil peanut butter ★ birdseed

7. Place peanut butter and birdseed inside the can.
8. Hang the feeder outside.

THE FEEDER

1. Ask an adult to remove both ends of a large can (a). Remove the label if any.
2. Push a long cord through the can. Knot the ends together (b).
3. Push a shorter cord through the can. Knot the ends close to the can (c).
4. Tape real or artificial leaves to the can (d).
5. Cut daisies from colored paper. Make a hole in each flower with a pencil.
6. Tie the flowers to the ends of the shorter cord (e).

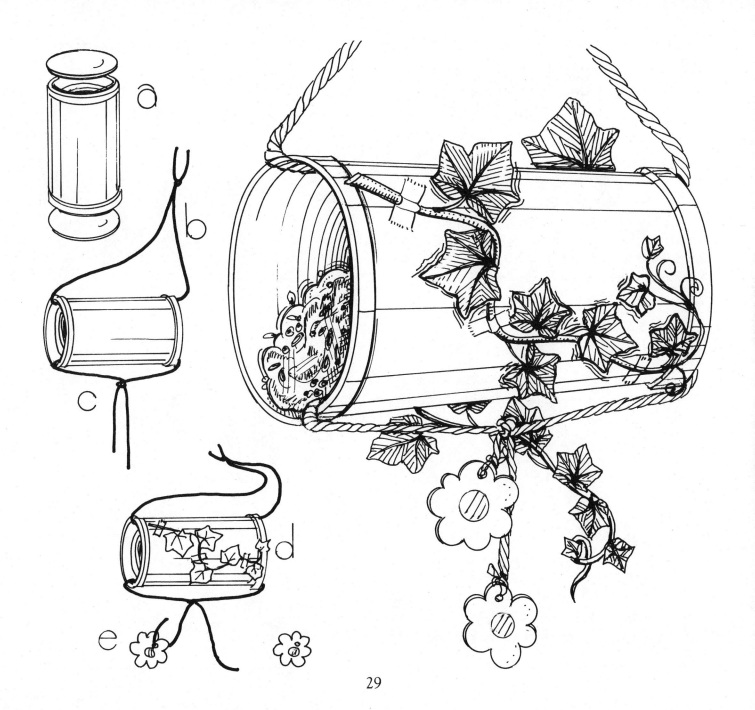

Palace Guard

It is the palace guard's job to watch over the king and queen's palace. The guard is stationed in a guardhouse and he wears a colorful uniform, like a fancy wooden nutcracker soldier. Here's your own personal palace guard who will keep watch over *your* palace—your room, that is.

THE GUARD

1. For the hat and the upper body, cut two blue papers as tall as the two large cans and long enough to wrap around them. Tape both in place (a).
2. For the face, cover a smaller can in a skin-color paper. Draw on a face and hair.
3. For the legs, cover the remaining cans in yellow paper.
4. Glue the head on the hat (b). Dry.
5. Glue the other end of the head to the body (c). Dry.
6. Cut two arms from blue paper. Glue on skin-color hands (see arrows in d).
7. Glue the arms to the back of the body (d).
8. Glue a paper feather to the hat, epaulets to the arms, and crisscrossing strips to the body (e).
9. Tape the yellow cans together.
10. Glue the taped cans to the body.
11. Cut one end of the straw at an angle in each of about four drinking straws (f).
12. Push the pointed ends of the straws into the uncut ends to form a pole.
13. Tape a paper flag to the pole.
14. Tape the pole to one hand. Fold the other arm up to make your guard salute.

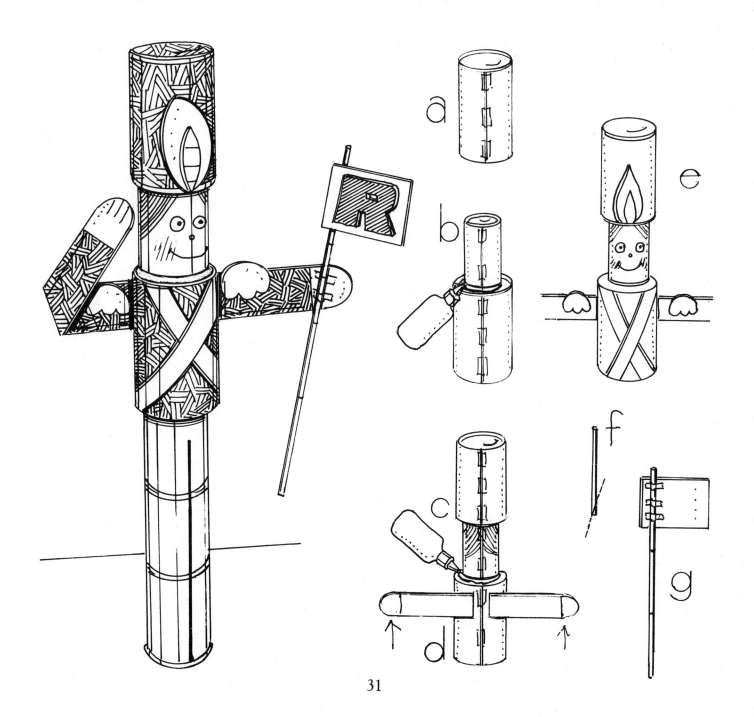

Rhythm Shakers

Rhythm shakers are fun to play because you don't have to learn how to read music. Just turn on the radio or stereo and shake them to the beat of your favorite songs.

People in Brazil and Portugal shake maracas to music. Maracas are very much like rhythm shakers. They are made from hollow gourds filled with dried beans or seeds.

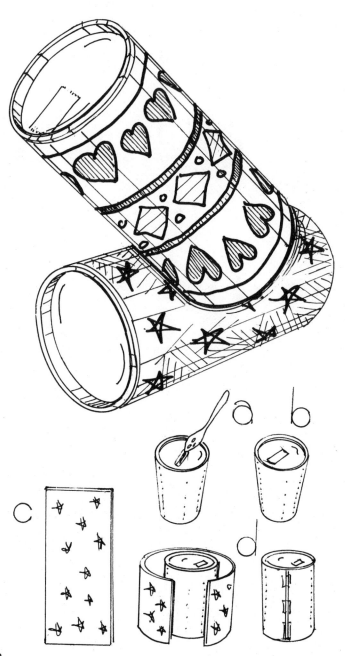

THINGS YOU NEED
two aluminum soft drink cans
colored paper ★ dried beans or lentils
tape ★ crayons or markers

THE SHAKERS

1. Ask an adult to help you remove the tabs from the aluminum cans by bending them back and forth.
2. Spoon some dried beans or lentils into the cans (a).
3. Tape over the openings (b).
4. Cut a piece of paper as tall as each can and long enough to wrap around it.
5. Draw designs on the papers with crayons or markers (c).
6. Wrap the papers around the cans. Tape both into place (d).

32

PAPER PLATES

Sun Catcher

A sun catcher will bring a rainbow of colors into your room. When held up against a window or a light, it looks like a stained-glass window. Go wild with geometric patterns or design something simple, like a teddy bear or a sailboat.

THE SUN CATCHER

1. Draw shapes on the underside of a plate (a).
2. Cut out the drawn shapes (b).
3. Cut a tissue paper circle large enough to cover the cutout designs (c).
4. Spread paste on the inside of the plate around the cutout designs (d).
5. Press the tissue onto the pasted plate.
6. Color the tissue paper over each cutout design with a different color marker (e).
7. Make a hole near the edge of the plate with a paper punch or a pencil.
8. Tie string into the hole.
9. Hang your sun catcher from the string in a window, with its underside facing you.

THINGS YOU NEED
paper or foam plate ★ colored markers drawing or white tissue wrapping paper paper punch or pencil ★ string scissors ★ paste

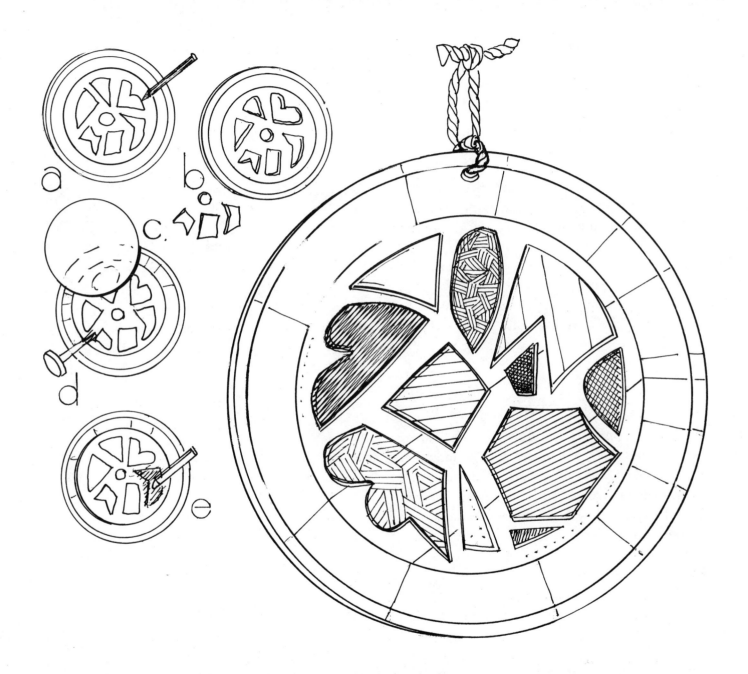

35

Animal Faces

What are your favorite animals? Here are four wonderful creatures found in different parts of the world. Pigs are found all over the world; lions in Africa and southern Asia; owls in North and South America, Europe, and Asia; and pandas in China. The pig, lion, owl, and panda will look nice hanging on your bedroom wall. Make as many animal faces as you can think of, and invent some friendly beasts of your own.

THE PANDA, PIG, OWL, AND LION

1. Draw the animals' features on colored paper. The panda (A) has black ears, eyes, and nose. The pig (B) has a red mouth, pink ears, pink nostrils, and green or brown eyes. The owl (C) has a yellow beak, brown feathers, and grey eyes. The lion (D) has a red mouth, yellow eyes, a pink nose, and pink cheeks.
2. Cut out the drawings.
3. Paste the cutouts for each animal on the underside of a plate. Use a bowl for the pig.

THINGS YOU NEED
plastic, foam, or paper plates and bowls colored paper ★ scissors ★ crayons or markers ★ yarn ★ white glue ★ paste

4. Draw on crayon or marker details, like the panda bear's smile and the owl's feathers.
5. Paste the ears or feathers for each animal to the inside of the plate.
6. Glue on yarn for the lion's mane.

A

B

C

D

37

Hanging Coils

If you want to decorate your room with some really festive things, make a bunch of hanging coils. These springy decorations have a hypnotic effect, especially if they are spinning. Decorate them with really unusual designs. Hang them by an open window on a breezy day, or turn on a fan and watch them spiral 'round and 'round.

THINGS YOU NEED
lightweight paper plates ★ pencil ★ scissors crayons or markers ★ white glue ★ glitter button ★ string

THE COILS

1. Twist a sharpened pencil through the center of a plate (a).
2. On the underside of the plate, draw an overall design (b), one that goes from the center to the edge (c), or glue on glitter (d). You can also draw designs or glue on sequins after the plate has been cut into a spiral.
3. Cut into the plate following a spiral line (e). Stop cutting a little way from the center hole. Study the large circle with the dotted spiral line.
4. Tie a button to the end of a piece of string (f).
5. Push the other end of the string through the hole (g). The button should be on the inside of the plate (g).
6. Hang the plate by the string to form the coil.

a

b

c

d

e

f

g

39

Four-String Banjo

"Oh, I come from Alabama with my banjo on my knee . . ." That's the way the song from the United States goes.

The banjo is an American musical instrument with a plunky, plucky sound. Afro-American slaves introduced the banjo in the 18th century to America. The banjo makes this sound because its strings are played against a plastic or skin head. Bluegrass and country music bands use the banjo. Make this plunky musical instrument and accompany yourself to traditional songs like "O Susanna" or "Down in the Valley."

THE BANJO

1. Cut a long, narrow rectangle from cardboard for the banjo's neck. It should be more than twice as long as a plate. You can use corrugated cardboard from food cartons that you can get at a food market or grocery.
2. Draw lines across the neck for the banjo's frets (see the arrow in a).
3. Make four holes into each end of the neck by twisting a sharpened pencil through the cardboard (a).
4. Cut two slits into the plate (shown by the lines in b).

THINGS YOU NEED
corrugated cardboard ★ scissors ★ pencil
crayons or markers ★ two plates the same size
colored paper ★ white glue ★ cord

5. With the underside facing up, slip the neck through the slits (c).
6. Turn the plate over.
7. Glue the neck to the inside of the plate (d).
8. Squeeze glue on the entire plate rim (e).
9. Press the rim of the other plate onto the glued rim. Let it dry.
10. Cut four small ovals from colored paper for the banjo's keys. Glue them to the top of the neck (see the arrow in f).
11. Cut a length of cord or yarn that is four times the length of the neck plus a little extra. Knot one end.
12. To make the banjo's strings, weave the cord up and down the bar. Start at the first hole at the top and end at the last hole at the top. Then make another knot and trim away the extra cord.

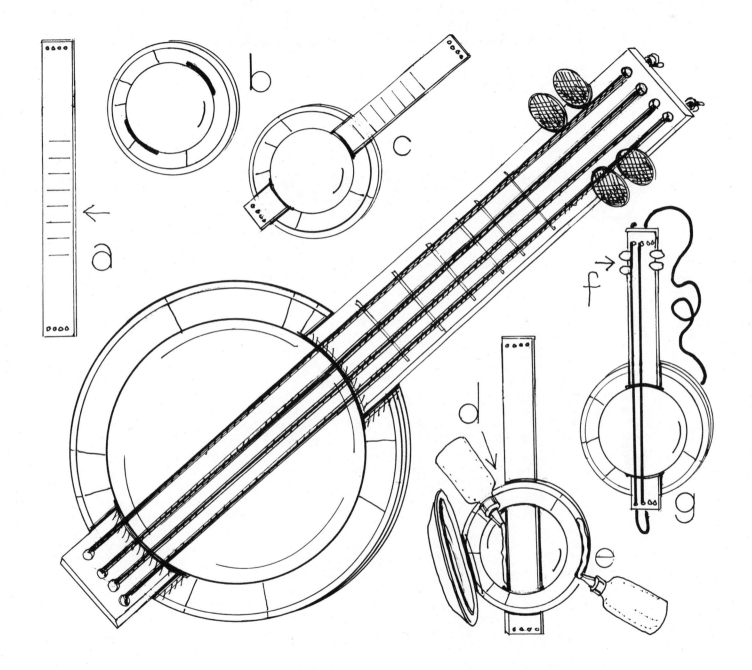

41

Happy Cherry Pie

Open up this pie and you will see a gang of happy cherries. To make it, all you need are two brightly colored plates and a lot of smiling faces to add to the fruits. You can also make a pie with sleepy blueberries, angry apples, or singing strawberries.

THINGS YOU NEED
two paper or foam plates the same size
crayons or markers ★ red and pink paper
scissors ★ paste

THE PIE

1. Draw air holes shaped like raindrops on the underside of one plate (a).
2. Cut a circle from pink paper as large as the inside bottom of the other plate.
3. Draw cherries with smiling faces on red paper. Cut them out.
4. Paste the cherries on the pink circle (b).
5. Spread paste on the inside bottom of the plate (c).
6. Press the pink circle onto the paste.
7. Place the plate with the air holes on top of the plate with the cherries to form the pie.

a

b

c

d

Paper Plate Fans

Fans are not only pretty to look at, but they provide a refreshing breeze on a hot summer day. Little plates make little fans, and big plates make spectacular fans. Make a collection to decorate your room, or make one for each family member to help him or her stay cool during summer months.

THE FANS

1. Cut away the bottom of a paper plate to create a handle. Follow one of the three designs shown in the drawing.
2. Ask an adult to help you punch a hole into the handle with a paper punch.
3. Draw a design on the underside of the plate with crayons or markers.
4. Tie a ribbon into the hole and make a bow.

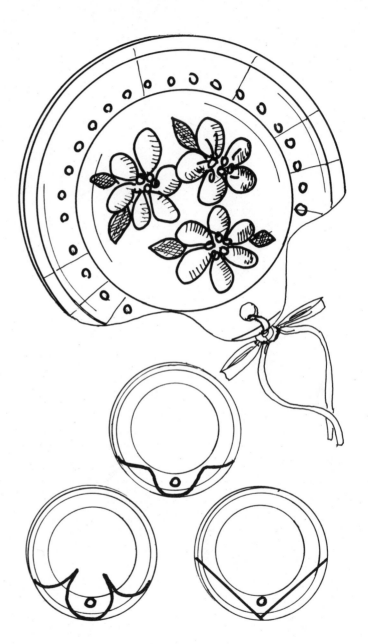

44

JARS

Monkey Bank

A fat piggy bank is a familiar shape for storing money. Now is the time to be a little different. Deposit all your spare pennies, nickels, and dimes into this monkey bank. The larger the jar, the more money you'll be able to save for that rainy day.

THINGS YOU NEED
brown and pink paper ★ crayons or markers
large glass jar with lid
paste ★ scissors

THE BANK

1. Draw a face on brown paper that will fit on a large glass jar. Also draw two round ears (a).
2. Cut out the face and ears.
3. Cut two small pink circles. Paste them to the ears (b).
4. Remove the label from the jar with warm water.
5. Paste the face to the jar (c).
6. Fold over a little bit of each ear (d).
7. Paste the folded side of the ears to the jar, on each side of the face (e).
8. Ask an adult to punch out a money slot in the lid.
9. Screw the lid on the jar.

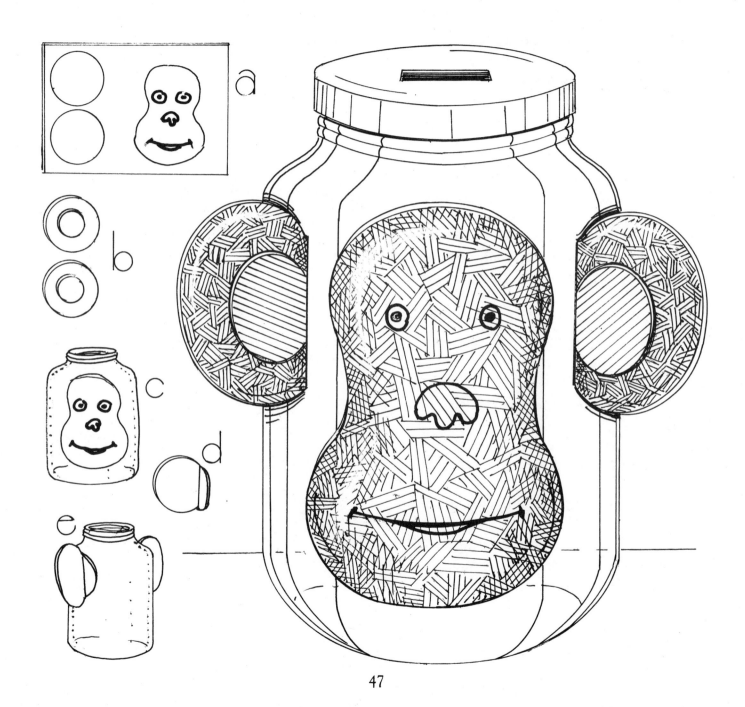

a

b

c

d

e

47

Terrarium

A terrarium is a glass container in which you grow all kinds of plants. First, add dirt. Second, plant seedlings and water them well. Third, screw on the lid and place the terrarium by a window or a bright light. The only thing left to do is watch your plants grow. Sprinkle in water only if the dirt looks dry.

It's good for the Earth and for people, too, when green things grow.

THINGS YOU NEED
large glass jar ★ small stones ★ potting soil seedling plants

THE TERRARIUM

1. Use warm water to remove the label from a large jar.
2. Add a small layer of little stones to the jar (a). You can use driveway gravel or garden pebbles.
3. Fill one-third of the jar with potting soil (b).
4. Add small seedling plants to the soil (c).
5. Sprinkle water into the jar until the soil is wet. Do not over-water.
6. Ask an adult to punch holes in the lid.
7. Screw the lid on the jar.

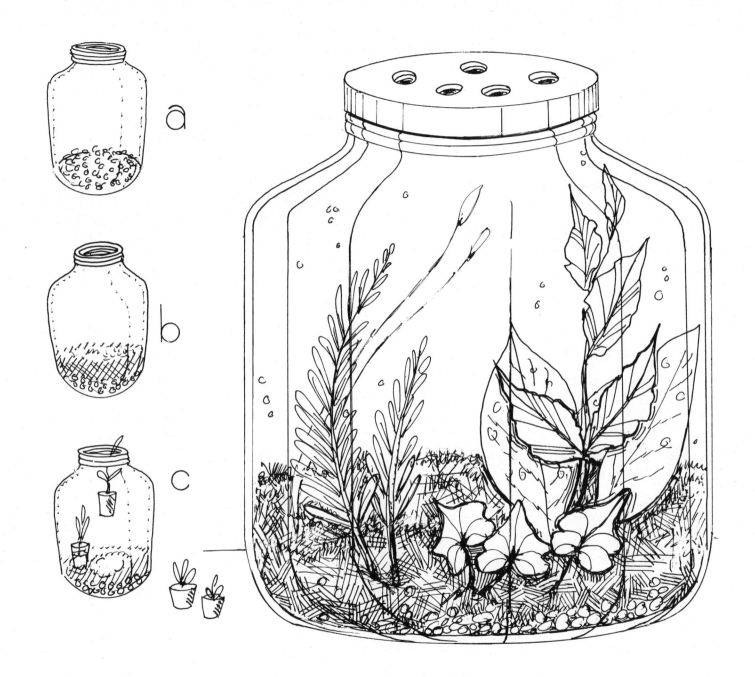

a

b

c

49

Snow Globes

A snow globe is a glass or plastic container with a scene in it. Usually a snow globe is filled with water and glitter. When you shake the globe, it looks like a blizzard inside. Make snow globes with your favorite small possessions in them. They are fun to watch, and they make great gifts for your friends and family.

THINGS YOU NEED
glass jars ★ plastic knickknacks and flowers water ★ food coloring ★ glitter and sequins spoon

THE SNOW GLOBE

1. With warm water, remove the label from a jar.
2. Put plastic items, glitter, and sequins into the jar (a).
3. Half fill the jar with water (b).
4. Add a few drops of food coloring to the water. Stir with a spoon.
5. Fill the jar to the rim with water.
6. Screw on the lid tightly.
7. Shake the jar and turn it upside down. Rest the jar on its lid to see the glittery blizzard.

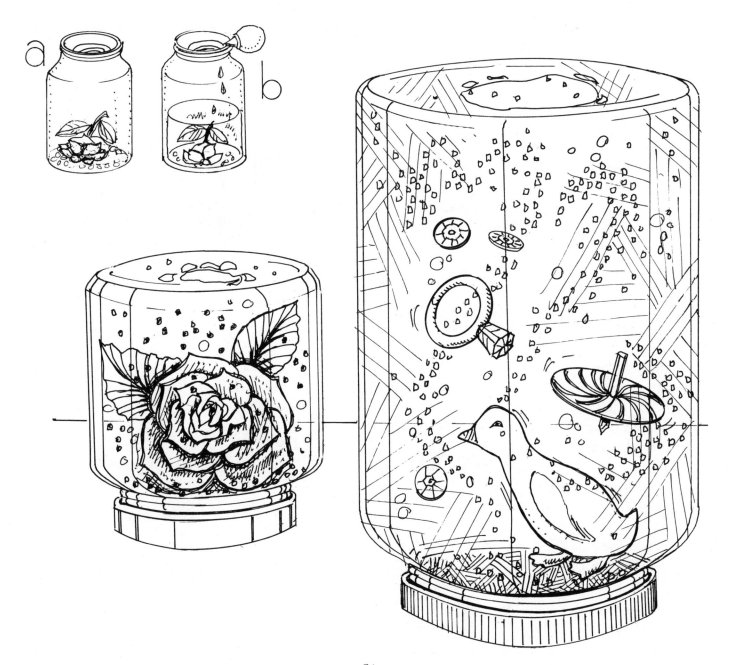

51

Candle Holders

Candle holders make great presents for your mom, dad, grandma, or grandpa. They are easy to make, and you can be creative with all kinds of glitter, sequins, and plastic flowers. Be sure that only adults light the candles.

THINGS YOU NEED
two small glass jars ★ plastic flower
white glue ★ candles ★ glitter and sequins

THE CANDLE HOLDERS

1. Use warm water to remove the labels from two jars the same size.
2. Place a plastic flower upside down in one jar (a).
3. Screw the lid on the jar.
4. Stand the jar on its lid. The flower will drop onto the lid.
5. Squeeze a lot of glue onto the bottom of the jar (b).
6. Press the bottom of the other jar onto the glue.
7. When the glue has dried, place a candle inside the top jar.
8. For decorated candle holders, squeeze glue around the jars (c). Sprinkle glitter onto the glue. Glue on sequins.

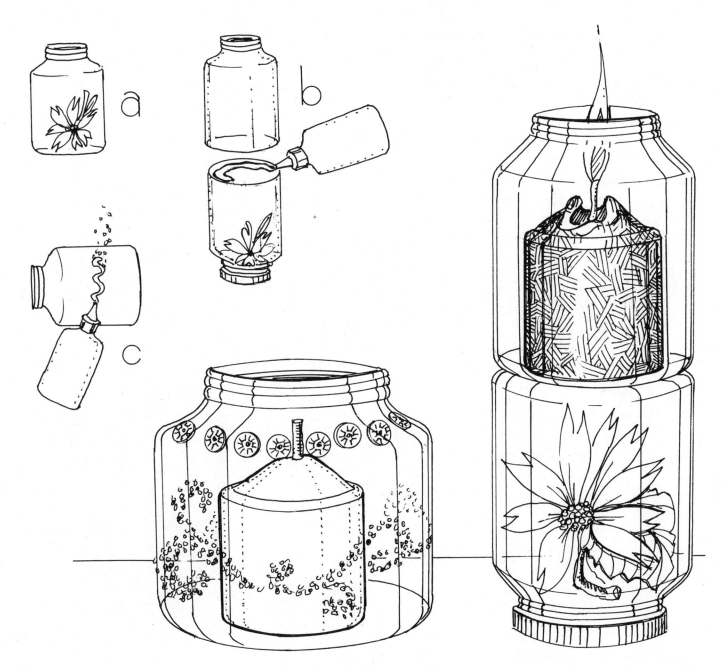

a

b

c

53

Time Capsule

Make a time capsule and put inside a letter you write and a small collection of special things. Set a date when your time capsule is to be opened. Bury it in your backyard, or give it to an adult to hold for you. When your time capsule is opened, let's say ten or fifteen years from now, out will come a flood of childhood memories.

THINGS YOU NEED
large glass jar with lid ★ sheet of paper
pencil or pen ★ special treasures
clingy plastic kitchen wrap

THE TIME CAPSULE

1. Use warm water to remove the jar's label.
2. Write a letter to yourself on paper to be read when you are a grown-up.
3. Roll up the letter and tie it with string.
4. Place the letter inside the jar. Also add your special things.
5. Place a piece of clear plastic wrap over the open end of the jar before you screw on the lid very tightly.
6. Bury the time capsule in your backyard, or give it to an adult to keep for you until the big day you have chosen to open it.

PLASTIC BOTTLES

Clown Marble Roll Game

You need keen eyes to play the clown marble roll game. Each player gets ten marbles. Set the smiling clown on the floor a good distance away from the shooting line. In turn, each player rolls or shoots the marbles at the clown's bow tie. The one who gets the most marbles in is the winner.

THINGS YOU NEED
large (gallon or 4-litre) bleach bottle
colored paper ★ scissors ★ tape
paste ★ marbles

THE MARBLE GAME

1. Ask an adult to thoroughly rinse out a large bleach bottle. Remove the label from the bottle.
2. Ask an adult to cut out a big, round opening in the front of the bottle at the bottom (a).
3. Cut a nose, mouth, eyes, and cheeks from colored paper. Also cut out two sides of a bow tie.
4. Paste the face on the bottle (b). Paste the sides of the bow tie to opposite sides of the hole.
5. Roll colored paper into a cone that fits over the top of the bottle, covering the handle. Tape the cone in place (c).
6. To make the hat, trim the cone so that the bottom edge is even (d).
7. Cut two pieces of colored paper for the hair. Cut slits into them.
8. Paste the hair to the inside of the hat (e).
9. Place the hat on the bottle, and you're ready to roll.

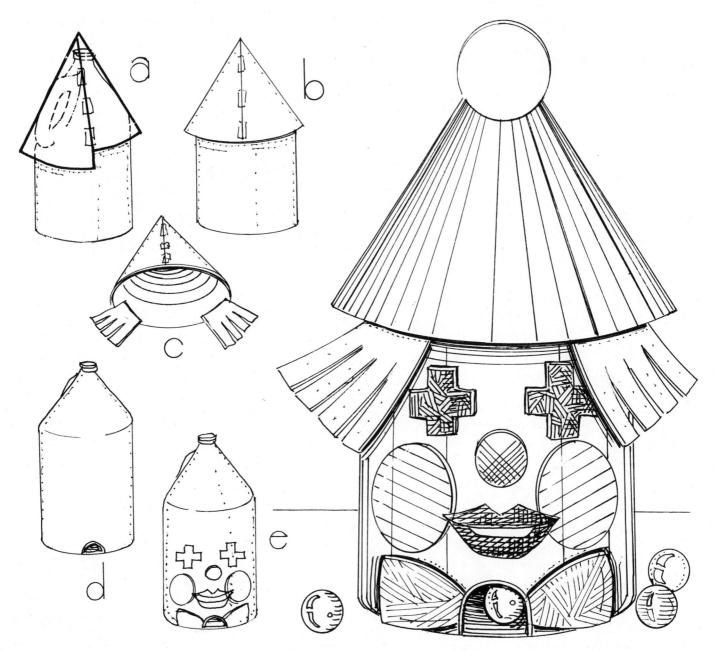

a

b

c

d

e

Scene in a Bottle

Building model sailing ships in bottles is a very old craft. Each piece has to be carefully glued in place through the small opening. It takes a long time to finish even the smallest boat.

But *you* can create a scene in a bottle very easily. All you have to do is arrange all sorts of miniature things on cardboard and place the bottle over it. You could make a sports scene for your dad or a holiday scene for your mom.

THE SCENE

1. Remove the label from the bottle.
2. Ask an adult to cut out a long oval opening on the side of the bottle (a).
3. Cut out a piece of cardboard larger than the cutout oval.
4. Glue small items to create a miniature scene on the cardboard. They should be close together so that the opening of the bottle can fit over them (c). Instead of a scene, you could glue on blocks, toy soldiers, a toy ship, or whatever you like.
5. Squeeze glue completely around the edge of the opening of the bottle (c).
6. Carefully place the glued opening over the scene and onto the cardboard (d). Let the bottle dry.

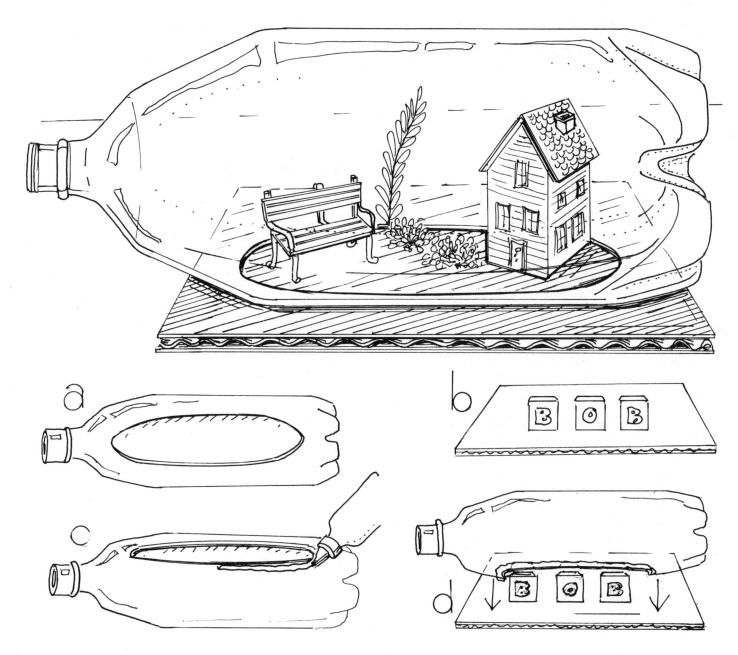

Friendly Scarecrow

You may not have a cornfield in your backyard or on your street, but that doesn't mean you cannot own a scarecrow. This handsome, friendly farm hand couldn't even frighten a chickadee, let alone a crow. But he would be a fine addition to your room. Use your imagination and create a paper cornfield to make him feel at home.

THINGS YOU NEED
cardboard ★ yarn ★ scissors
liquid detergent bottle ★ paintbrush ★ cord
outdoor paint ★ stick ★ white glue

THE SCARECROW

1. Wrap yarn many times around a piece of cardboard (a).
2. Tie all the yarn together at one end (b).
3. Cut away the yarn at the other end (c).
4. Tie the yarn together a little way down from the first knot to form a tassel (d).
5. Make three more tassels.
6. Have an adult thoroughly rinse out a plastic detergent bottle.
7. Remove the label from the bottle with warm water.
8. Paint a face on the bottle with the neck at the bottom (e).
9. Glue two tassels to the top of the bottle (f).
10. Push a stick into the bottle. You can use a tree branch or a broom handle.
11. Tie two tassels around the neck of the bottle (g).

Bowling

When you can't get to the bowling alley, you can turn your home into one. The pins are plastic bottles and any large ball will make a good bowling ball. A long hallway is ideal for an alley.

Play the simple version of the game. In turn, each player gets two chances to knock over the ten bottles. This is called a "frame." The person who knocks over the most pins in ten frames is the winner. Set up the pins and start bowling.

THE PINS

1. Remove the labels from ten large soft drink bottles.
2. Paint numbers from 1 to 10 on the bottles with house paint.
3. Stand the bottles in four rows with a little space between them. Row one has one pin, Row two has two pins, Row three has three pins, and Row four has four pins. The pin numbers should be in order.

THINGS YOU NEED
ten plastic soft drink bottles all the same size ★ outdoor or indoor paint ★ paintbrush ball

Indoor Lawn

Growing a lawn in your room is fun whether you have a backyard or you live in a city. The thickness of your grass depends on how much seed you plant in the dirt in a soft drink bottle. It will take a little "tender loving care" and patience to get a healthy lawn. You have to make sure the dirt doesn't get too dry. By the way, mowing the lawn won't be one of your chores.

> **THINGS YOU NEED**
> large plastic soft drink bottle ★ funnel
> spoon ★ potting soil ★ grass seed ★ water

THE LAWN

1. Spoon potting soil into a bottle through a funnel (a).
2. Sprinkle grass seed into the bottle (b). Shake the bottle a little so that the seeds mix in with the soil.
3. Add a few spoonfuls of water to moisten the soil.
4. Place the bottle by a window. Add water when needed. The grass will begin to grow in about ten days.

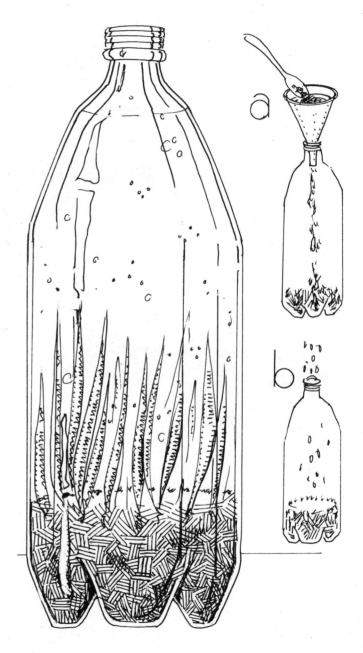

clockwise from top:
*Christmas Tree Ornaments
(p. 174), Valentine's Day
Heart (p. 158), Easter
Bunny (p. 164), Birthday
Cake (p. 154), Jar
Pumpkin (p. 166)*

A

Jack-in-the-Box (p. 124)

International Doll (p. 66)

B

Time Capsule (p. 54)

Weather Station (p. 100)

C

left to right: *Clown Marble Roll Game (p. 56), Jumbo Dice (p. 102), Big Top (p. 74)*   top inset: *Paper Plate Fans (p. 44)*

D

left to right: *Arbor Day Tree (p. 162), Gingerbread House (p. 94)*

E

left to right clockwise: *Slowpoke Turtle (p. 108)*, *Chipmunk on a Stump (p. 88)*, *Know Your Earth Quiz Show (p. 179)*

F

top from left to right: *Bag of Flowers*
(p. 22), *Bird Feeder (p. 28)*, *Terrarium*
(p. 48)

left: *Wild West Fort (p. 92)*, *Snow*
King & Queen (p. 70)

G

left to right: *Life-Size Palm Tree (p. 261), Totem Pole (p. 14), Plastic Flatware Sunburst (p. 148)*

H

CUPS

International Dolls

There are many countries on this big planet called Earth. You may not be able to visit all these countries. But with this collection of international dolls, you can bring the children of the world into your home. Just let your imagination fly away to India, Japan, Mexico, or Kenya.

THE HEAD

1. Blow up a small round balloon no bigger than a baseball (a).
2. Squeeze white glue into a paper cup.
3. Tear newspaper into tiny strips.
4. Place a newspaper strip on waxed paper.
5. Paint the top of the strip with glue (b).
6. Lay the glued side on the balloon (c).
7. Cover the entire balloon with strips, overlapping them (d).
8. Dry overnight.
9. Paint the balloon skin color (d).
10. Paint on a face (e).
11. For the hair, glue on tied lengths of yarn to the head (f). You can also use cotton, paper, or pompons.

THE BODY

1. Cut out the bottom of a paper cup (g).

THINGS YOU NEED
small round balloons ★ newspaper
white glue ★ small and large paintbrushes
waxed paper ★ poster paints ★ paper cups
scissors ★ colored paper ★ drinking glass
yarn ★ tape or paste

2. Wrap colored paper around the cup and tape in place (h).
3. Trim away the paper at the top and bottom of the cup (i).
4. Cut out paper arms. Glue them to the back of the cup (j).

ASSEMBLING THE DOLL

1. Rest the top of the head on a drinking glass (k).
2. Place the smaller end of the body on the balloon neck side of the head (l).
3. Squeeze glue into the body around the head (m). Allow it to dry.
4. Decorate the doll with paper cutouts shown in the drawings—Spain (A), Japan (B), Mexico (C), Africa (D), India (E), Morocco (F), Hawaii (United States) (G).

A

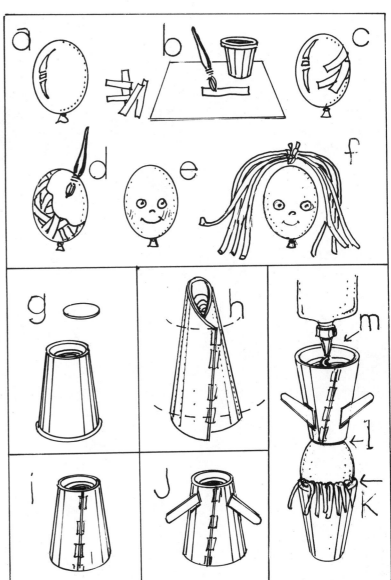

a

b

c

d

e

f

g

h

i

J

m

l

K

E   F   G

Snow King & Queen

After a blizzard, the countryside looks like a snowy white kingdom. The snowdrifts look like castle walls. And snowmen and snowwomen are everywhere. What is missing from this scene are the Snow King and Snow Queen. Make this royal couple and turn your room into a winter wonderland every day of the year.

THE KING AND QUEEN

1. Cut a pointed design into the rim of two cups to make the crowns (a).
2. Draw a face on each cup (a).
3. Glue a cup with a face to the bottom of an uncut cup (b).
4. Cut white paper into strips for the hair. Cut slits into the strips (c).
5. Glue hair around the head below each crown (d).
6. Cut four arms from paper. Glue two to each cup (e).

71

Pop-up Puppet

The pop-up puppet is like a turtle. Its head can disappear into its body. Just raise and lower its drinking-straw body. Make a cast of characters and put on a puppet show for your friends or family. After the final bows, retire your pop-up actors to their paper cup bodies until the next show.

THE PUPPET

1. Cut one end of a drinking straw at an angle (see the dotted line in a).
2. Push the pointed end of the straw into the other straw (b).
3. Draw an oval head with a smiling face on paper. Cut the head out.
4. Tape the attached straws to the back of the head (c).
5. Glue yarn or cotton hair to the back of the head, covering the straw (d).
6. Glue a little hair to the face (e).
7. Cut scrap fabric as tall as the cup and long enough to wrap around it, plus a little extra.
8. Wrap the fabric around the open end of the cup. Hold the fabric in place with a rubber band (f).
9. Twist a sharpened pencil through the bottom of the cup.
10. Push the straw with the head attached through the fabric and out the hole in the cup (g).
11. Gather the fabric under the head and tie it tightly to the straw with cord (h).

73

Big Tops

Round and round they go. Where they stop, nobody knows.

Tops are fun to play with, especially when they have geometric designs. Just imagine how much fun you will have with these jumbo tops. Give them a good spin and watch them whirl about the floor, like flying saucers landing on Earth. See how long you can make them spin.

THE TOP

1. Draw a small X in the middle of a piece of poster board (see the arrow in a).
2. Set the point of a compass on the X. Draw a circle about the size of a dinner plate (a). Cut out the circle.
3. Draw a design on the circle with crayons or markers (b).
4. Sharpen a new pencil, but do not make the lead too pointy (c).
5. Carefully twist the point of a new, sharpened pencil through the bottom of a foam cup (d) and through the *x* in the circle (e). The point should extend about as long as your thumb.

6. Glue or tape the cup to the circle.
7. To spin, give the pencil a good twist and let the top spin on its pencil point on a flat surface.

a

b

c

d

e

75

Game of Skill

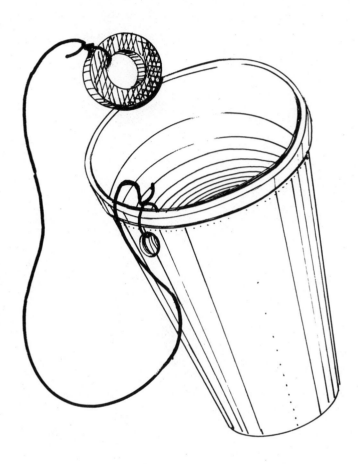

How well can you do with your hands what you see with your eyes? Sounds confusing. Well, here's a game of skill that answers that question. All you have to do is swing the rubber washer attached to a length of cord up into a paper cup. It may sound easy, but try it first. Good luck.

THINGS YOU NEED
paper cup ★ pencil ★ cord ★ rubber washer

THE GAME

1. Twist a sharpened pencil through a paper cup, near the top (a).
2. Cut a piece of cord twice as tall as the cup.
3. Tie one end of the cord into the hole (b).
4. Tie the other end of the cord to a washer.

BOXES

Shadow Box Window

What's your favorite season? Summer is the time to go to the beach or to the mountains. Winter is for throwing snowballs and ice skating. Spring comes alive with pretty flowers. And autumn explodes in bright colors.

Now you can enjoy your favorite season anytime of the year. All you have to do is to peek into a window shadow box. You can look at an icy winter scene when it's very hot outside. Or you can brighten up a damp, rainy day with an autumn country scene. Be sure to draw some happy winter pictures of sleds, skaters, snowmen, or whatever you choose.

THE SHADOW BOX

1. Draw a rectangle on the front of the cereal box a little in from the sides (a). Use a ruler to draw straight lines.
2. Cut out the rectangle (b). This creates a frame.
3. Cut four narrow strips from paper. Two fit from side to side. Two fit from top to bottom.

THINGS YOU NEED
cereal box ★ crayons or markers ★ ruler
scissors ★ colored paper ★ paste ★ tape

4. Paste the shorter strips to the frame (c).
5. Paste the longer strips to the frame, over the shorter strips (d).
6. Cut out four more strips. Glue them on the frame (e).
7. Draw an outdoor scene with crayons or markers on paper that will fit inside the box.
8. Spread paste on the back of the drawing (f).
9. Slip the drawing inside the box through the open end (g). The drawing should be seen through the window.

Hickory Dickory Dock

As the nursery rhyme goes, the grandfather's clock bonged so loudly it scared the tiny mouse. Down, down it ran. It was a good thing it was only one o'clock. Imagine how frightened the mouse would have been if it had been twelve o'clock.

If you like this rhyme, you can make it come to life. The clock's hands move so that it can be any hour of day. And the mouse is not afraid of loud bongs since the clock is its home. Time will fly when you are Hickory Dickory Docking.

THE CLOCK

1. Tape the open end of a cereal box closed.
2. From a grocery bag, cut a piece of paper as tall as the box and long enough to wrap around it (a).
3. Tape the paper to the box.
4. Trace around the bottom of the box on the same paper (b). Cut out.
5. Paste the paper to the top of the box (c).
6. Cut a circle from colored paper. Draw on a clock's face (d).
7. Cut out two clock hands from colored paper.

THINGS YOU NEED
small cereal box or small box ★ scissors large brown paper grocery bag ★ tape pencil ★ paste ★ colored paper ★ string crayons or markers ★ paper fastener

8. Push a paper fastener through the ends of both hands (e). Push the fastener through the center of the clock's face (f). Open it at the back (g).
9. Paste the clock's face to the box near the top (h).
10. Paste on a rectangle and a pendulum (h).
11. Cut a small slit into the side of the box (see arrow in i). Ask an adult to help you.
12. Draw a mouse on paper. Add a tab attached to the feet to fit into the slit on the box (i). Cut out and paste on a string tail.
13. Insert the tab into the slit.

Retro-Rocket Robot

Robots are machines that can do a lot of things people do. They can move from one place to another, pick up objects, and even talk. This robot may not be able to lift its arms or recite the alphabet, but it will be fun to play with.

Since there are boxes of all sizes and shapes, you can make an endless collection of robots. Some may be tall, some very small, others short and fat. With their aluminum foil covering, they will look real. Just move them along and give them electronic voices. And don't forget to give your robot friends some space-age names like Zeenon or RDT–47.

THE ROBOT

1. Choose a large box for the body, a medium-size box for the head, a small box for the power pack (candy box), and two square-end boxes for the legs. Cut a large toothpaste box in half for the legs.
2. Tape all the boxes' open ends closed.
3. Paint the boxes with silver or grey paint. You can also cover them with foil. Study a, b, and c.

THINGS YOU NEED

assorted boxes ★ tape ★ aluminum foil scissors ★ pencil ★ large plastic bottle caps white glue ★ plastic forks ★ colored paper

4. Glue the power pack to the body near the top. Glue on bottle caps (d). Let the glue dry completely.
5. Glue the legs to the bottom of the body (e). Dry.
6. Glue the head to the body (f). Dry.
7. Glue a bottle cap to the side of the body (g).
8. Glue a plastic fork to the bottle cap for an arm (h). Dry.
9. Glue on a second bottle cap and fork.
10. Glue on paper eyes, mouth, and nose.

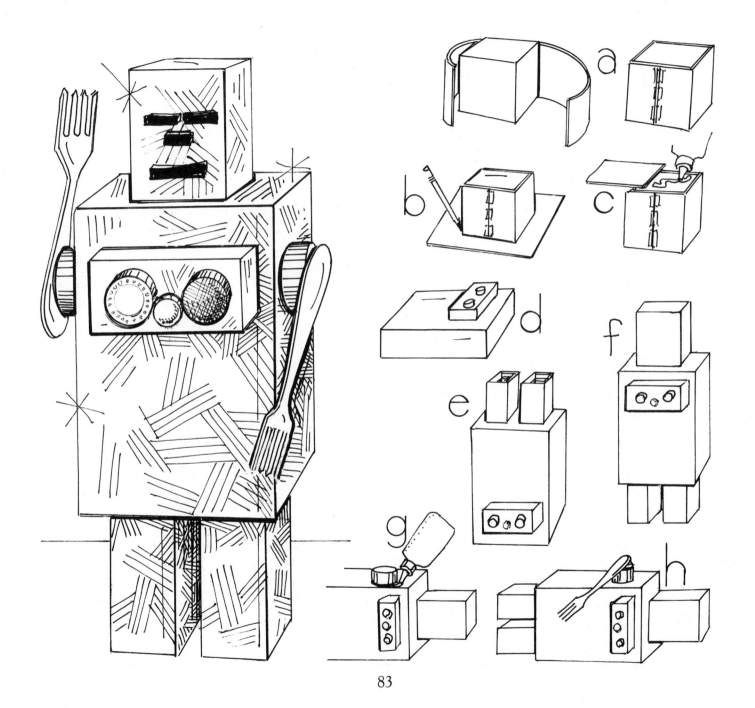

King Arthur's Castle

Imagine you are one of the Knights of the Round Table back in the 6th century. These knights were honorable and gracious. They lived in King Arthur's castle in Britain. They wore a shiny suit of armor and carried a long sword.

You could make your own suit of armor, and here's how to design your own castle. Make your fortress complete with a drawbridge, towers, and colorful flags.

Invite your friends over and make them all knights. Wage a friendly war against friends who don't recycle. Spread the word that throwaways have to recycled. It's the only noble thing to do.

THE CASTLE

1. Tape the open end of the box closed.
2. Trace all sides of the box on paper (a). Cut out.
3. Draw bricks and windows on all sides.
4. Paste the sides to the box (b).
5. Cut paper as tall as several round boxes and tubes and long enough to wrap around them. Tape all in place (c).
6. Cut long strips from paper for the top of the

THINGS YOU NEED
large rectangular box ★ tape ★ colored paper
pencil ★ scissors ★ crayons or markers
paste ★ salt or oatmeal boxes
cardboard tubes ★ drinking straws

castle. Cut a notched design into one side of each strip. Study the design in the drawing.
7. Paste the strips to the top of the box (d).
8. Roll paper into cones large enough to fit over the cardboard tubes and round boxes. Tape them in place (e).
9. Trim the bottom of each cone evenly (f).
10. Cut drinking straws in half. Paste a triangle flag to each (g).
11. Cut off a tiny bit of the tip of each cone. Push a straw flag into each (h).
12. Draw a door at the bottom of the box (dotted line in i).
13. Cut along the lines to make the drawbridge (j). Ask an adult to help you.
14. Stand the round boxes and tubes at the sides and on top of the box to create the castle.

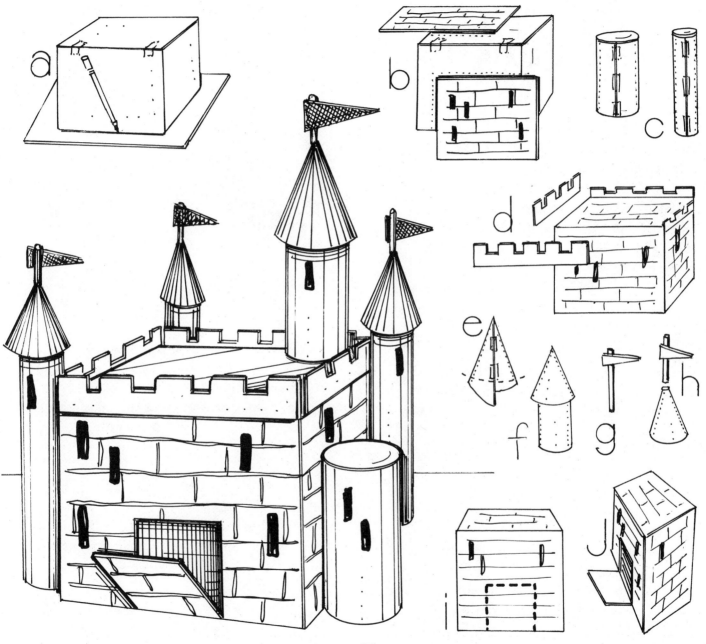

Giant Pencil

You know how fast your pencils wear down in class or when you are doing your homework. Here are some giant pencils that will last forever.

Make a collection of giant pencils in different lengths. Stand them in a corner of your bedroom or hang them on the wall above your desk. You can bring one to school to show your teacher and fellow students. By the way, it is OK to wear down your real pencils. That's why your parents and teachers give them to you.

THE PENCIL

1. Roll white or beige paper into a cone large enough to fit over a salt box. Tape the paper in place (a).
2. Color the tip of the cone with a black marker (a).
3. Trim the bottom of the cone evenly. The cone should be a little larger than the top of the box (study b).
4. Cut slits close together around the edge of the cone to form tabs (c).
5. Place the cone on top of the box. Fold the tabs onto the box. Glue down (d).

6. Cut yellow paper as tall as the box and long enough to wrap around it (e).
7. Tape the paper in place (f).
8. Cover the other two salt boxes as you did the first. Cover another one in yellow paper and the other in pink (g).
9. Trace around the bottom of the pink box on pink paper (h). Cut the circle out.
10. Glue the pink circle to the top of the pink box (i).
11. Glue a white paper strip around the bottom of the pink box (j).
12. Glue the boxes together with the pink box at the top and the pointed box at the bottom (k).

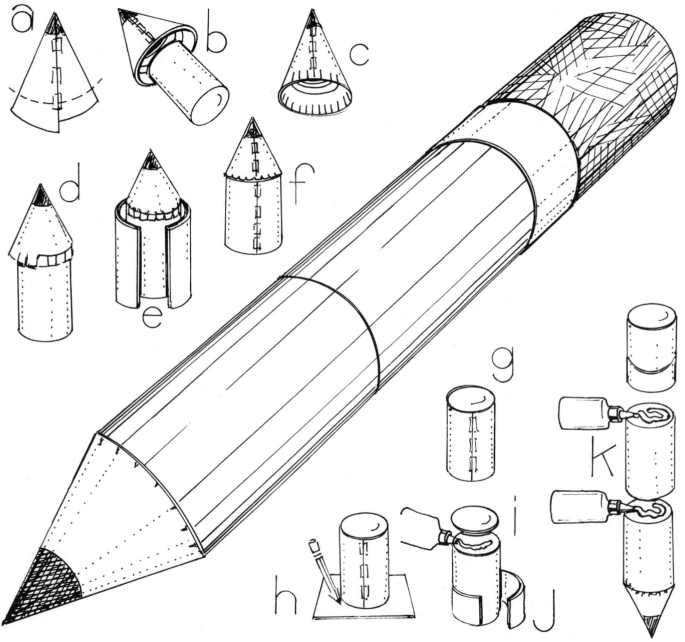

a

b

c

d

e

f

g

h

i

J

k

Chipmunk on a Stump

Chipmunks are so cute, especially when they are eating. They sit up on little hind legs and chomp their food very quickly. Sometimes their cheeks are all puffy with nuts which they take to their underground burrows or hide for the winter.

Preserve this natural scene with a chipmunk on a stump. Real chipmunks take long naps inside their burrows during the winter months, but your forest friend will be with you all year long. Find it a special place in your room. And remember, you don't have to feed it.

THE STUMP

1. Cut beige or light brown paper as tall as the box and long enough to wrap around it.
2. Draw a bark design on the paper with crayons or markers (a).
3. Wrap the paper around the box. Tape the paper in place (b).
4. Trace around the bottom of the box on the same color paper (c). Cut out.
5. Draw a spiral on the circle (d).
6. Paste the circle to the top of the box (e).

7. Draw leaves on green paper and cut them out.
8. Paste the leaves to the back of the box at the bottom (f).

THE CHIPMUNK

1. Cover a small can with paper just as you did the box (g).
2. Paste a large chipmunk tail to the back of the can (h). Paste two ears to the chipmunk's head.
3. Draw the chipmunk's hands, face, and feet on the front of the can.
4. Have your chipmunk sit on the tree stump.

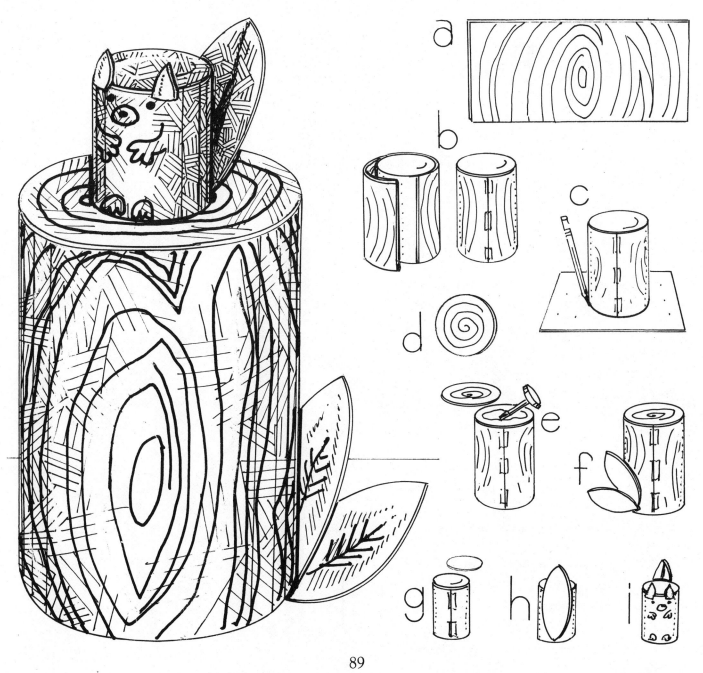

a

b

c

d

e

f

g h i

Comic Book File Box

Do you have a comic book collection? Do you have a hard time finding your favorite comic books? If you keep them in these special file boxes you will always know where they are. You can stand them on your bureau or on a shelf. But you need to get in the habit of putting your comic books back into their files when you finish reading them. That way, you'll keep everything neat.

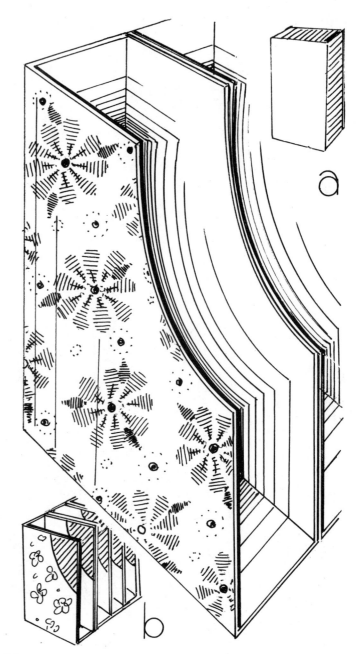

THINGS YOU NEED
three or more cereal boxes ★ glue ★ paste
gift wrapping paper ★ scissors

THE FILE BOX

1. Cut away the opened tops and one long side of the cereal boxes (see shaded areas in a).
2. Glue the boxes together.
3. Cut wrapping paper to fit on the outer sides of the glued boxes.
4. Paste each paper to its matching side.
5. Cut away the corners of the glued boxes in curved lines (see shaded areas in b).
6. Stack comic books inside the file box.

CARTONS

Wild West Fort

During the days of the Wild West in North America, forts stood across the new territories, just as many countries have army bases today. Your fort will be constructed in two parts, a courtyard for horses and a tower for soldiers. Be prepared. You never know when a band of outlaws might wander into your room.

THE FORT

1. For the courtyard, cut away the peaked top of one carton (see the dotted lines in a). Also cut away one side (see the shaded area in a).
2. Trace around one side of the carton on brown paper (b). Cut out.
3. Paste the paper sides to the carton (c).
4. Cut out a zigzag design along the top edges of the carton (d).
5. Draw lines on the sides with a crayon or marker to make a tall fortress fence (e).
6. For the tower, cut away the peak of the second carton. Cover it with brown paper as you did the courtyard.
7. Draw a door on two sides (see the dotted lines in f).
8. Cut along two lines of one door. Fold it open (g). Cut away the other door completely.
9. Tape the courtyard to the tower on the side with the cutaway door.
10. Tape a paper flag to a drinking straw.
11. Tape the straw to a corner of the tower.

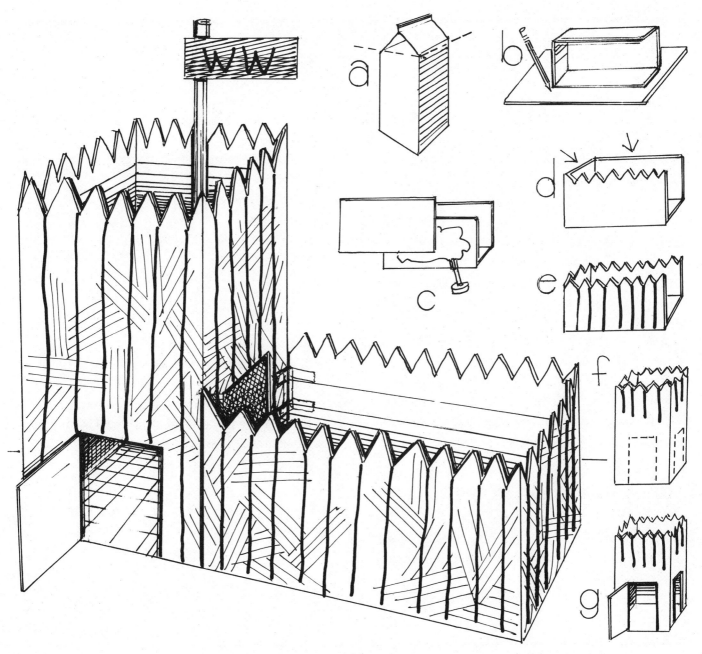

WW

a

b

c

d

e

f

g

93

Hansel & Gretel & the Gingerbread House

When Hansel and Gretel were lost in the woods, they stumbled upon a gingerbread and candy house. It looked delicious enough to eat and live in forever. But a wicked witch owned the house. The witch soon captured Hansel and Gretel. She wanted to fatten them up and have them for dinner. But Gretel outwitted the witch, so they managed to escape and found their way back home.

Act out this popular German folktale. Add your favorite candies to your gingerbread house. A strange place may be very tempting, but there is still no place like home. And a body cannot live on candy alone! Maybe next you could make a healthy fruit and vegetable house.

THINGS YOU NEED
peaked carton ★ scissors ★ tape ★ stapler
large brown paper grocery bag
colored paper ★ crayons or markers
white glue

THE GINGERBREAD HOUSE

1. Open the top peak of the carton.
2. From a brown paper grocery bag, cut paper as high as the opened carton and long enough to wrap around it (a).
3. Wrap the paper around the carton. Tape it in place (b).
4. Fold the top of the carton back into a peak. Staple the peak closed (c).
5. Fold a piece of red paper in half for the roof. Cut it to fit over the peak (d).
6. Decorate the house with windows, a door, shutters, and colorful candies. Use crayons or markers or paste on paper cutouts.
7. Glue the roof in place.

a

b

c

d

Noah's Ark

Noah had a big chore. He had to collect two of every kind of animal in the world and bring them aboard his ark. If he didn't, the rain that flooded the land would kill all the animals.

Noah's ark was like a floating zoo. Fill up your ark with as many pairs of animals as you know. On a rainy day, pretend you are bobbing in the sea, waiting for the sun to shine and dry up the land.

THE ARK

1. Open the top peak of the carton.
2. Cut away one side of the carton. It should be a side that was folded into the peak (see the arrow in a).
3. Trace around a side of the carton two times on colored paper (a). Also trace around the bottom. Cut them out.
4. Paste the cutouts to their matching sides of the carton (b).
5. Fold the top of the carton back into a peak. Staple the peak closed (c).
6. Choose a medium-size box that will fit inside the carton.

7. Trace around all sides of the box on colored paper (d). Cut out.
8. Paste the cutouts to their matching sides of the box (e).
9. Place the box inside the carton.
10. Draw round windows on the box and on the carton with markers or crayons (f).
11. Fold a piece of paper for the roof. Cut it to fit over the box.
12. Put the roof on top of the box.

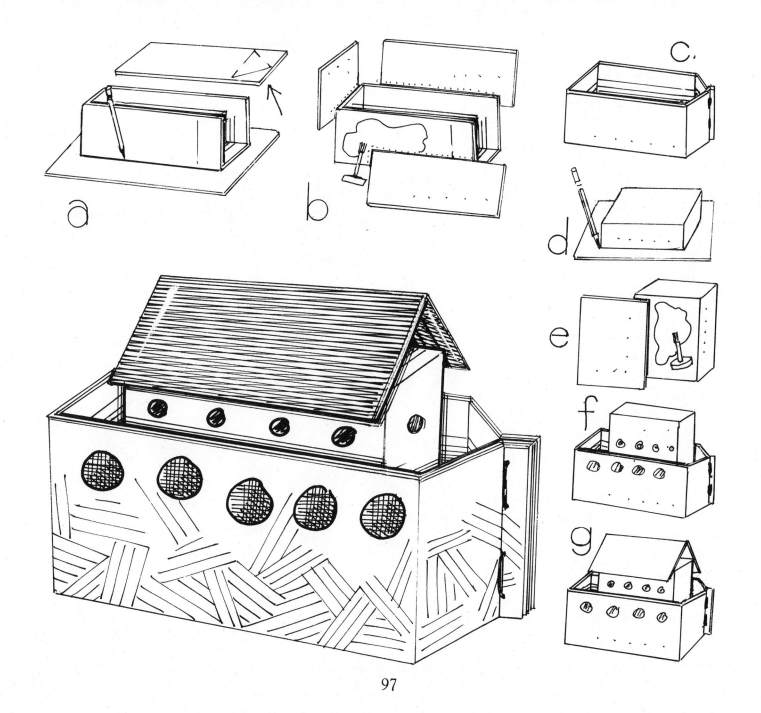

Traffic Light

Before you cross the street, you look at the traffic light. If the light facing you is red, you stay on the sidewalk. If it's yellow, you proceed carefully or wait until it turns green. If it's green, that means go—as long as no cars or trucks are coming. If that's confusing, this traffic light will help you remember.

THINGS YOU NEED
large brown paper grocery bag
peaked carton ★ scissors ★ tape ★ stapler
pencil ★ cord ★ colored paper ★ paste

THE TRAFFIC LIGHT

1. Open the peak of the carton (a).
2. From a grocery bag, cut paper as tall as the carton and long enough to wrap around it.
3. Tape the paper to the carton (b).
4. Fold the top of the carton back into a peak. Staple the top closed (c).
5. Carefully twist a sharpened pencil through the center of the peak (d).
6. Push a length of cord through the holes. Tie the ends together (e).
7. Cut four small red, yellow, and green paper circles.
8. Paste three circles on each side of the carton. Red is at the top, yellow is in the middle, and green is at the bottom.

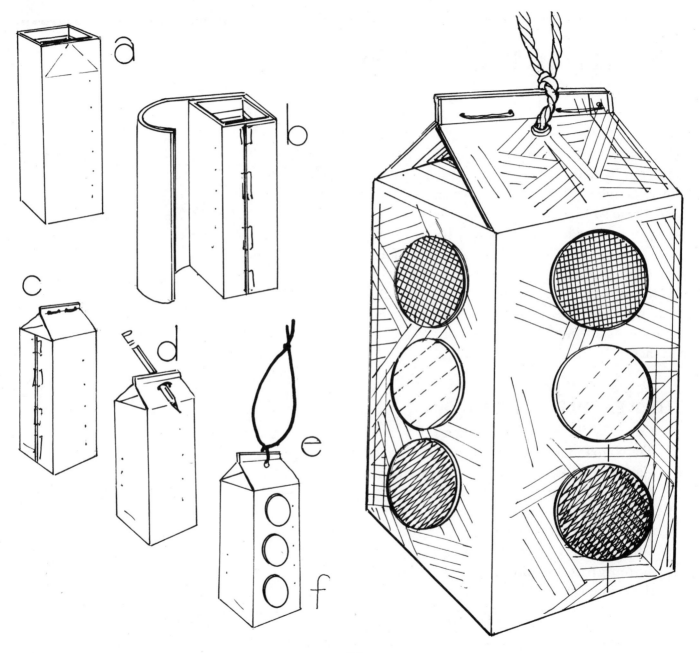

99

Weather Station

The best way to tell what the weather is is to look out your window. It may be sunny, cloudy, rainy, or snowy. Set up this weather station in your home so that your family can see what the weather is outside. You can also listen to the radio or television to see what the weather forecasters are predicting.

Meteorologists are scientists who study the weather. They look at clouds, air pressure, temperature, and more to figure out the day's weather.

THE WEATHER STATION

1. Cut away the peak of the carton (a).
2. Trace around a long side of the carton four times on drawing paper (b). Trace around the bottom. Cut the pieces out.
3. Draw a design on each paper for SUN, CLOUDS, RAIN, and SNOW.
4. With the opened end of the carton at the bottom, paste the drawings and the top to the carton (c).

Jumbo Dice

The next time you and your friends play a board game, surprise them with a pair of jumbo dice. It will take two hands to throw them, but there will be no question about what number you threw.

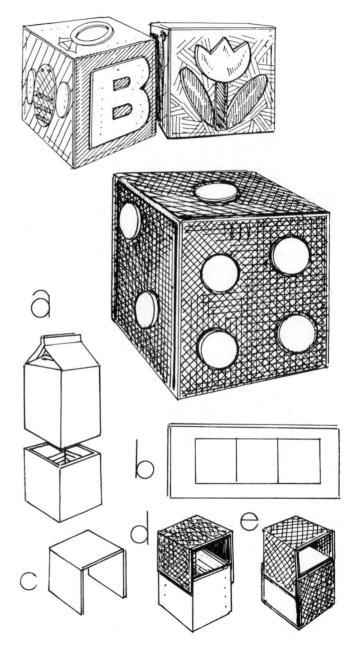

> **THINGS YOU NEED**
> two peaked dairy cartons ★ scissors ★ crayon
> black and white paper ★ paste ★ large coin

THE DICE

1. Cut away the top of a peaked carton to make a square box (a). It should be just as tall as it is wide.
2. Trace around the bottom of the box three times in a row (b). Make two rows.
3. Cut out the two rows. Fold them along the drawn lines (c).
4. Place one folded paper over the open end of the box (d). Paste it in place.
5. Place the other folded paper on the remaining sides of the box (e).
6. Trace around a coin on white paper twenty-one times. Cut out the circles.
7. Paste the circles on all six sides of the box just like real dice. Make another die.
8. You can also make building blocks.

DAIRY CONTAINERS

Flowerpot

Imagine drawing one flower on a piece of paper, and like magic it turns into a bouquet. The trick is to fold a sheet of paper like an accordion and cut out a flower, leaving some of the folded sides attached.

Make this pretty pot and arrange your paper flowers in it. Give the flowerpot to someone special at home or to your favorite teacher. If you want to keep it for yourself, set it on the windowsill in your room or keep it on your desk.

THE POT

1. Mix poster paint and a little cleanser in a paper cup. The cleanser will make the paint stick better.
2. Paint the dairy container to make the flowerpot.
3. Cut out a paper bow. Paste it to the flowerpot.

THE FLOWERS

1. Fold an entire sheet of paper back and forth like an accordion (a).
2. Draw a circle at the top of the folded paper

THINGS YOU NEED
dairy container ★ poster paints ★ pencil paintbrush ★ white paper ★ scissors yellow paper ★ paste ★ kitchen cleanser

for the flower. Draw a long bar from the circle to the bottom of the paper for the stem (b).
3. Draw a petal design around the flower and two leaves on the stem (c). The leaves must include some of the folded paper (see the arrows in c).
4. Cut out the flower, stem, and leaves (see the shaded areas in d). Do not cut into the folded sides of the leaves!
5. Open the paper.
6. Cut small circles from yellow paper.
7. Paste a circle in the middle of each flower (e).
8. Make more flowers.
9. Gather the flowers and place them in the flowerpot you made.

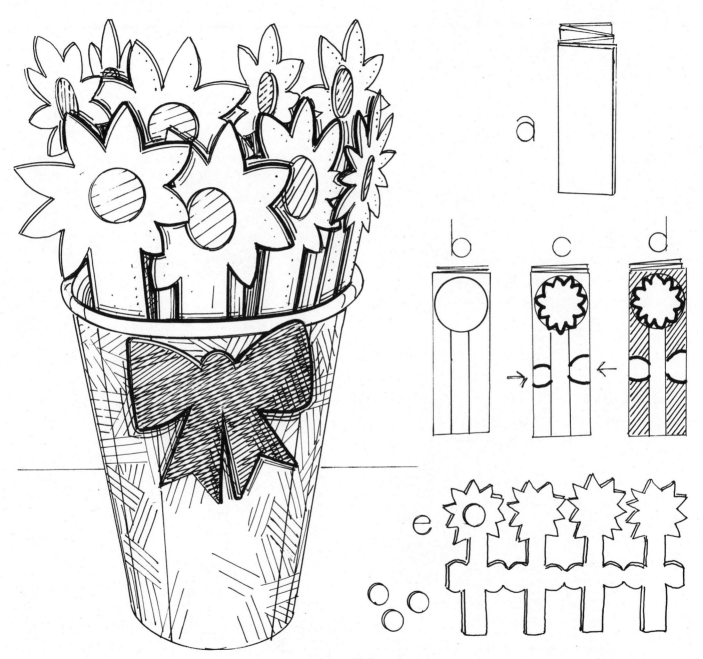

a

b   c   d

e

105

Yarn-Wrapped Basket

One way to decorate a container is to wrap yarn around it. Collect lengths of yarn in many colors. Start gluing on the lengths of yarn at the bottom of a dairy tub. Create bands of colors in all sizes. When you have reached the top, you will have a pretty container. You can use it to hold your marbles, beads, or paper clips. Make as many as you want. You'll be the most organized member of your family!

THINGS YOU NEED
large or small dairy tub ★ waxed paper
ribbon ★ white glue ★ paper cup
yarn or cord ★ scissors
paintbrush ★ colored paper

THE BASKET

1. Pour glue into a paper cup.
2. Paint glue around the bottom of a dairy tub, not too high up (a).
3. Cut several long lengths of yarn or cord. (It's OK to use all different colors.)
4. Wrap a length of yarn or cord around the tub, starting at the bottom (b). Press it into the glue as you wrap.
5. Keep brushing on glue and wrapping yarn around the tub, until you reach the top.
6. Cut out a paper handle.
7. Glue the ends of the handle to the inside of the tub (c).
8. Tie a bow to the top of the handle. Add Easter or fruit basket grass if you wish.

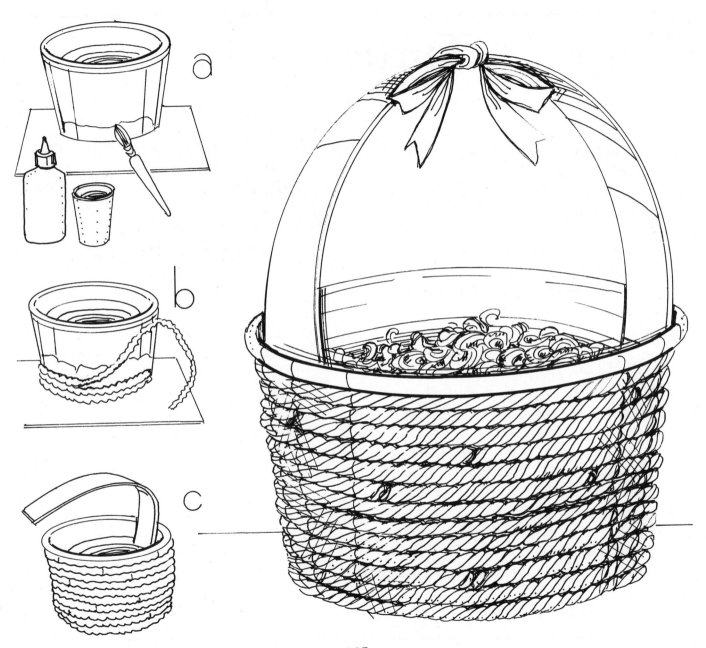

107

Slowpoke Turtle

Turtle characters are very popular in movies. Sometimes they have strange names. They wave long, shiny swords and chase away the bad guys.

Here's a cute turtle that moves slowly. Maybe that's because it carries its house on its back. It will go where you go. Give it a name, like George, Gerry, Larry, or Linda. You and your green pet will enjoy hours of peaceful play.

THE TURTLE

1. Mix light green poster paint and a little cleanser in a paper cup. The cleanser will make the paint stick better.
2. Paint the short, round container. When it is dry, paint on a dark green shell design.
3. Trace around the open end of the container on green paper (a).
4. Draw a head and a pointed tail opposite each other on the circle (b).
5. Add four feet with pointed toes to the circle (c).
6. Cut out the turtle shape (d).

7. Squeeze glue around the edge of the circle (e).
8. Place the open end of the container on the glue. Dry.

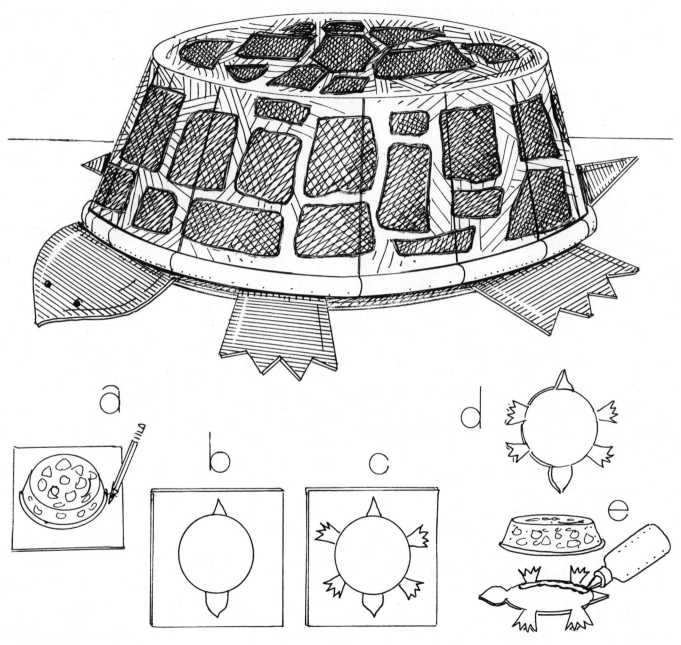

a

b

c

d

e

Loving Cup

"And the winner is . . ."

Loving cups are often presented to people who win a contest or a race. Sometimes they are given as a sign of appreciation. There must be someone in your life who could use such an award. If you think about it, you just may have to make more than one. Let's see. There's your mom, your dad, and don't forget your grandma and grandpa, and what about . . .

THE CUP

1. Wrap colored paper around the large container. Tape in place (a).
2. Cut away the paper around the top and bottom of the container (b).
3. Cover the medium-size container just as you did the large container.
4. Glue the bottom of the medium-size container to the bottom of the large container (c). Let the glue dry.
5. Draw two circles on colored paper with a compass. You can also trace around a coffee mug.

THINGS YOU NEED
large and medium dairy containers
colored paper ★ scissors ★ tape ★ white glue
compass ★ crayons or markers

6. Draw a line down the center of the circle (d).
7. Draw a half circle inside one half of the circle (e).
8. Cut the circles out to form the handles (shaded areas in f).
9. Fold the solid half of each handle in half (g).
10. Glue the handles near the top of the large container (g).
11. Write the words WORLD'S GREATEST and the name or the title of a special person on a piece of paper.
12. Glue the paper to the top of the loving cup.

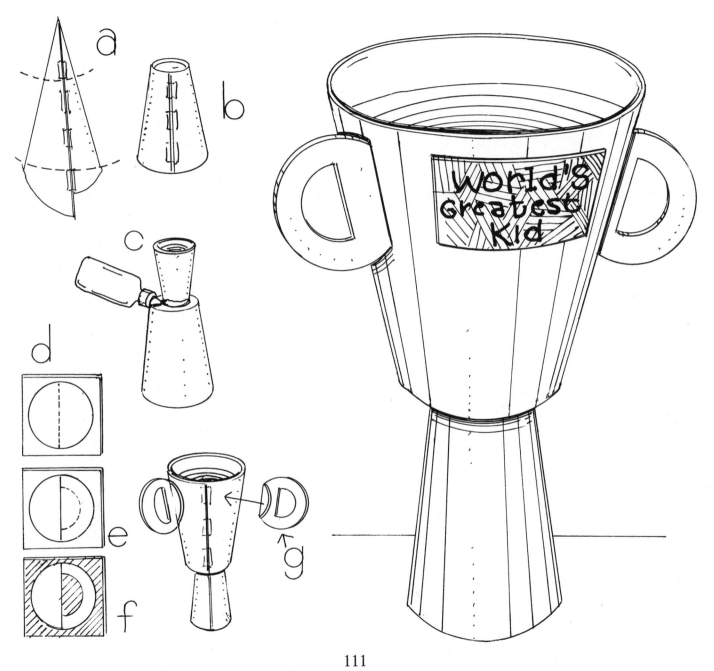

a

b

c

d

e

f

g

world's
Greatest
Kid

111

Ticktacktoe

Ticktacktoe (noughts and crosses) is a game played with pencil and paper. With this version, you can put away the writing tools and get right to the action.

The game board has four paper strips and ten yogurt containers are the playing pieces. There are two players. Choose who will be the X and who will be the O. In turn, each puts a letter in a space. The first player to get three X's or O's in a row—down, across, or diagonally—wins the game.

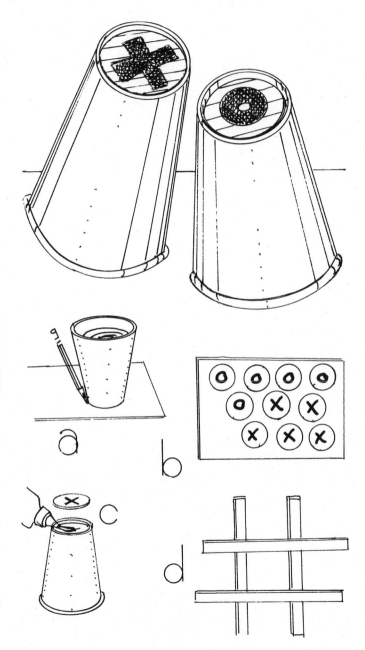

THINGS YOU NEED
ten small yogurt containers the same size
colored paper ★ pencil ★ scissors ★ white glue

THE GAME

1. Trace the bottom of a small yogurt container ten times on colored paper (a).
2. Draw an O on five of the paper circles and an X on the other five (b).
3. Cut out the circles a little bit smaller than the drawn lines.
4. Glue the circles to the cup bottoms (c).
5. Cut four long strips from colored paper.
6. Arrange the strips on a table (d) and begin the game.

EGG SHELLS

Blown Eggs

The next time your mother needs an egg or two in her baking or cooking, ask her to blow out the eggs so that you can recycle the shells. Collect blown eggs as they're used and store them in an egg carton until you are ready to make some very "egg-citing" crafts.

HOW TO BLOW OUT AN EGG

1. Twist a pin over and over into the narrow end of an egg until it breaks through the shell (a).
2. Twist the pin through the wide end of the egg (b).
3. Very carefully chip away a little bit of the shell at the wide end (c).
4. Blow very hard into the smaller hole until all the egg has been blown through the larger hole into a cup (d).

HOW TO DYE AN EGG

1. Wash a blown egg inside and out with cold water. Do not use soap.
2. Dye the blown eggs in egg dyes or food coloring. Add a little salt or white vinegar to the food coloring.
3. Dry eggs in an egg carton.

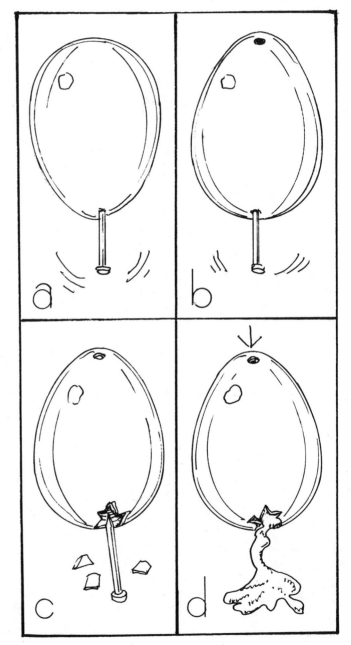

114

Circus Clowns

What is your favorite circus act? If your answer is the clowns, then you will enjoy this project. Make a troupe of clowns and clown heads. Then have a Big Top of fun. Ringmaster, blow your whistle to start the show. Let's bring in the clowns!

THINGS YOU NEED
blown eggs ★ food coloring or egg dyes
colored paper ★ white glue
large bottle caps ★ tape ★ scissors

THE CLOWNS

1. Dye blown eggs in bright colors.
2. Cut out hair, eyes, nose, and a mouth for each clown from colored paper.
3. Glue a face and hair to each egg.
4. Roll paper into small cones for the clowns' hats. Tape the hats in place (a).
5. Trim the bottom edge of the cones evenly (b). The cones should fit on the clown heads.
6. Decorate the hats with paper cutouts.
7. Stand the clown heads on large bottle caps.
8. Place the hats on the heads.

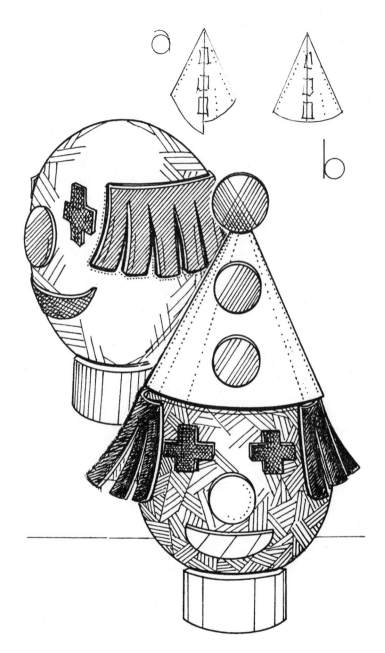

Jungle Animals

The animals that live in the forest are not the same ones that live in the jungle. Jungles are found in tropical places, and they are thick with vines, ferns, low bushes, and trees. That's where you will find lions, tigers, and elephants. These animals also live on open savanna—tropical flatlands. Make these three jungle friends, to roam around your room together.

THE ELEPHANT, TIGER, AND LION

1. Dye blown eggs in food coloring or egg dyes. (They can also be colored with wide-tip markers.) The elephant (A) is grey, the tiger (B) is orange, and the lion (C) is yellow.
2. Cut the ears, eyes, cheeks, mouth, and nose of the elephant, tiger, and lion from colored paper.
3. Glue each animal's features on its proper colored egg.
4. Glue yellow knitting yarn to the top of the lion's head. Glue broom straw whiskers under the noses of the lion and tiger.
5. Rest the animals on plastic bottle caps.

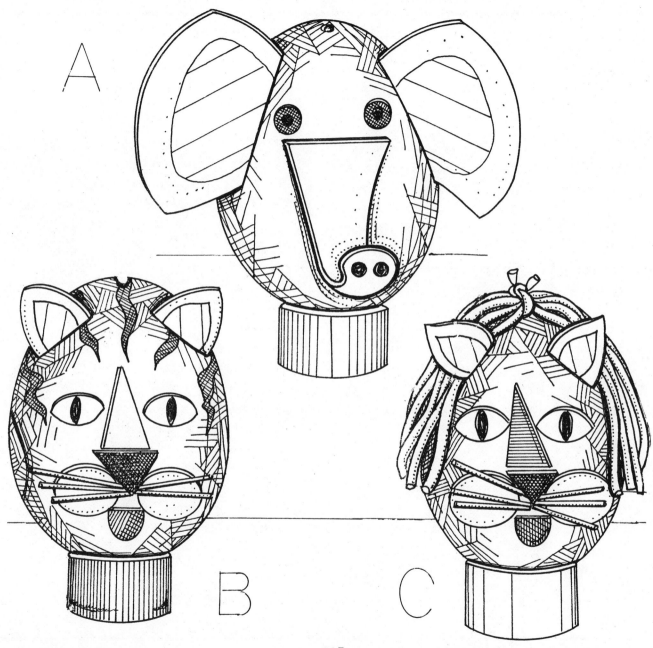

A

B

C

117

Wise Old Owls

In the animal kingdom, the owl is supposed to be the wisest bird of all. Maybe it just looks like it is wise, because owls have big eyes and look like they are wearing eyeglasses.

Owls search for food during the night. Make this forest friend and it will keep watch over you when you sleep. You'll never catch your owl with its eyes closed.

THE OWLS

1. Cut out a piece of brown paper that is as tall as the tube and long enough to wrap around it (a).
2. Draw a bark design on the paper with crayons or markers.
3. Tape the paper to the tube to form the tree stump (b).
4. Cut a circle from cardboard that is wider than the open end of the tube.
5. Place the stump on the circle. Glue it in place (c).
6. Cut eyes, wings, feet, head feathers, and a beak from colored paper. Paste them to a dyed, blown egg.
7. For the nest, glue cut-up knitting yarn or Easter or fruit basket grass on the stump, just below the owl.
8. Rest the owl on your stump. Let it dry.
9. For an owl in a nest, rest an owl on a large bottle cap that has knitting yarn or basket grass glued around it.
10. For a hanging owl, weave string through the holes of a button. Glue the button to the top of the owl. Hang.

119

Aliens from Outer Space

You'll look to the universe for this project. This alien and robot have travelled to Earth in their flying saucer from a planet far beyond Jupiter. Make them welcome guests in your home and find them a nice place in your room.

Before you begin to create these far-out beings, dye the blown eggs in outer space colors. The robot is grey or silver, and the alien can be any bright color. And the flying saucer? Just let your imagination travel beyond the Milky Way.

THE ROBOT (A)

1. Cut out the bottom of the cup (a).
2. Cut the cup in half (see dotted line in a).
3. Cut out a triangle (shown in b).
4. Cover the cut cup with a piece of aluminum foil.
5. Cut out arms and a power pack from colored paper.
6. Glue the arms and power pack to the back of a dyed blown egg (c).
7. Draw on a face. Add decorations to the power pack.
8. Stand the robot on the drinking cup.

THE ALIEN (B)

1. Draw a face on a dyed blown egg.
2. Cut arms and a belt with a buckle from colored paper.
3. Paste the belt around the middle of the alien. Paste the arms to the back.
4. Stand the alien on a bottle cap.

THE FLYING SAUCER (C)

1. Draw round windows on a dyed blown egg.
2. Weave a length of string through the holes of a button.
3. Glue the button to the flying saucer.
4. Hang your flying saucer when the glue is dry.

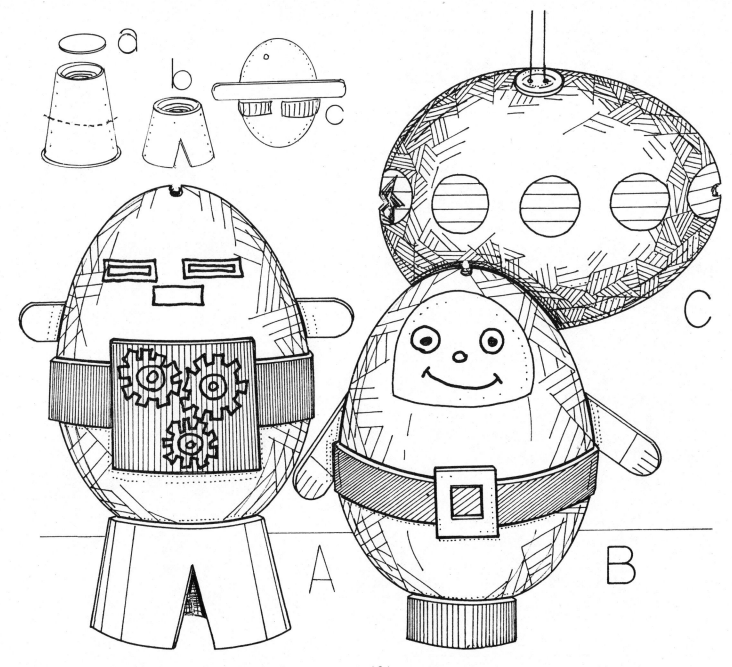

a

b

c

A

B

C

121

Summer Fruits

Apples, bananas, and pears are good to eat in the winter, but summer is the best time for strawberries, plums, and peaches. Make a bowl of fruit to remind you of the tastes and smells of summer. Even in winter, they will remind you of trips to the beach and sleeping late in the morning.

THINGS YOU NEED
blown eggs ★ food coloring or egg dyes
crayons or markers ★ green paper
drinking straws ★ paste
white glue ★ scissors

THE FRUITS

1. Dye blown eggs in fruit colors.
2. Draw on any details, like the seeds of a strawberry, with crayons or markers.
3. Cut out leaves from green paper.
4. Paste leaves directly to the fruits or to small lengths of drinking straws that have been glued to the egg.

TUBES

Jack-in-the-Box

The jack-in-the-box is a fun toy. Children have been playing with jack-in-the-boxes for over 300 years. They turned the crank and heard the tune "Pop Goes the Weasel." And at the "pop" in the song, the lid opened and Jack popped out. But all jack-in-the-boxes do not have music.

This Jack doesn't pop out of his box. But you can have fun with it or make one for a baby sister or brother. With a wave of his rattle, he will bring a smile to your face.

THE JACK-IN-THE-BOX

1. Cut away the top half of the carton (see the dotted lines in a).
2. Trace a side of the bottom half of the carton four times on colored paper with a pencil (b). Cut out.
3. Paste colored paper designs on one cutout side for the front of the box.
4. Paste all sides to the box (c).
5. Stand a tube inside the box that has been covered with colored paper. Squeeze glue around the bottom of the tube (d). Dry.

THINGS YOU NEED
medium peaked carton ★ scissors
colored paper ★ pencil ★ paste ★ toilet paper
cardboard tube ★ white glue

6. Cut out paper arms. Glue them to the back of the tube (e).
7. Cut out a paper head. Paste paper eyes, eyebrows, nose, and mouth on the head.
8. Paste the head to the top of the tube (f).
9. Cut out a hat, a collar, and a ball on a stick. Paste them on Jack.

a

b

c

d

e

f

g

125

Slinky Snake

The snake is not the most appreciated creature in the animal kingdom. That may be because snakes are rather scary looking. They have a long, slithering body, scaly skin, and a forked tongue. This slinky snake, however, is quite tame and makes a wonderful pet. It can be as long or as short as you want. Since snakes come in all sizes and colors, go wild with colors and designs.

THE SNAKE

1. Cut out colored paper as tall as a cardboard tube and long enough to wrap around it (a).
2. Draw a scale design on the entire paper with a crayon or marker (a).
3. Wrap the paper around the tube. Tape the paper in place (b).
4. Cover the other tubes the same way.
5. Cut out a circle for the snake's head from paper. It should be larger than the end of a cardboard tube. A heavy paper, like poster board, is best.
6. Twist two holes through the center of the circle with a sharpened pencil (c).

THINGS YOU NEED
eight or more toilet paper cardboard tubes
colored paper ★ scissors
crayons or markers ★ tape ★ pencil ★ cord

7. Cut a length of cord longer than the tubes when they are laid end to end.
8. Tie one end of the cord into the holes of the circle (d).
9. Feed the other end of the cord through all the tubes (e).
10. Tie the end of the cord from the last tube to a triangular tail (f).

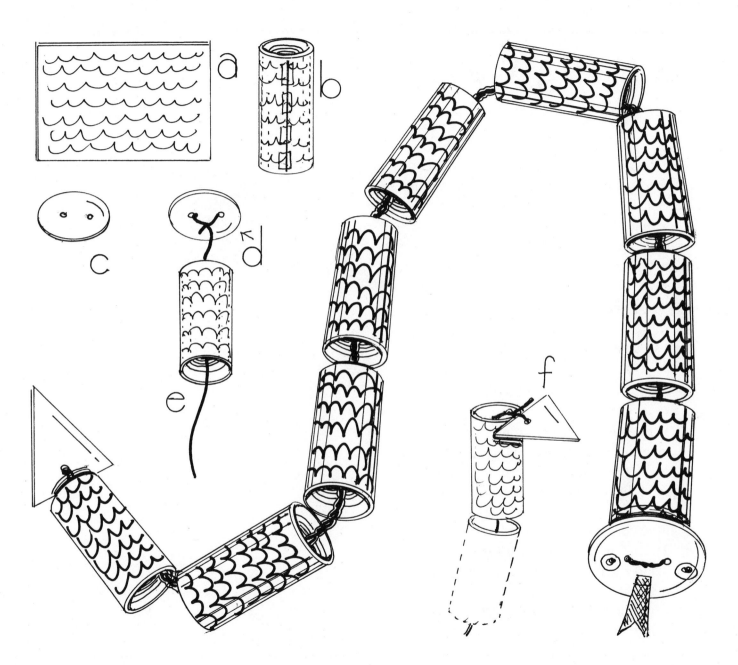

Roaring Campfire

There is nothing more relaxing than sitting in the woods at night in front of a roaring campfire. The next best thing is inviting your friends over for a camp out and sitting around this imitation log fire. Simply put a flashlight in the middle of the cardboard logs, turn off the lights, open the window, and tell ghost stories—just as if you were camping.

THINGS YOU NEED
six paper towel cardboard tubes
brown and red paper ★ pencil ★ cord
scissors ★ tape

THE CAMPFIRE

1. Cut brown paper as tall as a tube and long enough to wrap around it. Cut one for each tube.
2. Wrap the cut paper around each tube and tape in place to form the logs (a).
3. Make two holes into the top of each log by carefully twisting a sharpened pencil back and forth (see the arrow in a).
4. Feed cord through the holes of the logs (b).
5. Tie the ends of the cords together.
6. Stand the logs up as though you were building a fire.
7. Crumple red paper for the fire. Place the fire inside the group of standing logs.

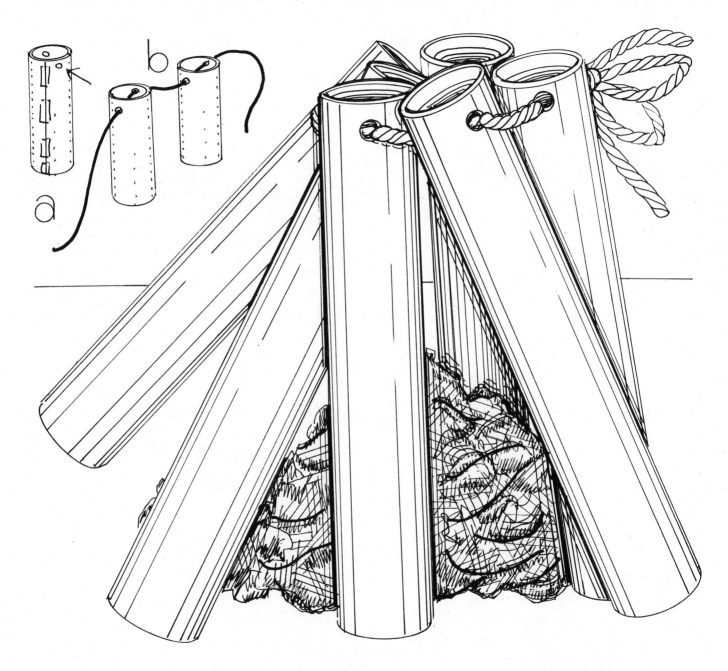

Robin Hood's Quiver

Return to those days of old England when Robin Hood and his merry men roamed the woods, helping those in need. According to legends, the outlaw Robin Hood robbed from the rich and gave to the poor. Whenever these expert archers were hungry, they drew their bows, took arrows out of their quivers, and hunted in the forest for deer, rabbits, and other animals for food. If *you* want a snack, all you have to do is go into the kitchen and raid the cookie jar. This quiver will give you hours of fun. You could imagine that your room is Sherwood Forest and that you are running away from the sheriff of Nottingham.

THE QUIVER

1. Cut out paper as tall as the tube and long enough to wrap around it.
2. Tape the paper to the tube (a).
3. Cut a paper circle larger than the end of the tube. Punch a hole in the center with a pencil (b).
4. Squeeze glue around the edge of the circle (c). Stand the tube on the glued circle. Dry.

THINGS YOU NEED

paper towel cardboard tube ★ brown paper scissors ★ tape ★ pencil ★ white glue ★ cord drinking straws ★ string

5. Push a length of cord through the hole in the circle and through the tube (d).
6. Tie the ends of the cord into a knot.
7. Cut a narrow paper strip as long as the tube. Cut slits into the paper to form a fringe.
8. Glue the fringe to the tube (e).

THE ARROWS

1. For each arrow, cut one end of a straw at an angle. Then push the cut end into an end of another straw (f).
2. Draw arrowheads on paper (g). Study the arrows in the quiver. Cut out your arrowheads.
3. Tie the arrowheads to the straws with string.
4. Put the arrows into the quiver and hang it around your neck.

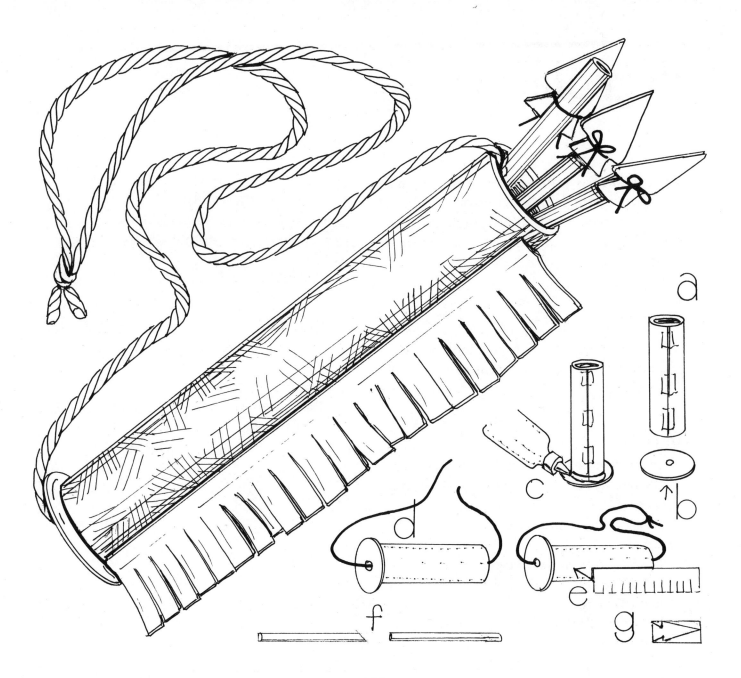

a

b

c

d

e

f

g

131

Flagpole

Since your room is your own territory, why not have your very own flag! Get creative and add all sorts of designs and words to a rectangle of fabric. Make a flagpole and proudly fly your personal banner.

THE POLE

1. Tape tubes together to form a long pole (a).
2. Glue a paper cutout ornament to the top of the pole.

THE FLAG

1. Cut a rectangle for the flag from a large piece of scrap fabric. It can be any color you choose.
2. Cut out three holes on a short side of the fabric (a).
3. Place the holes on waxed paper. Squeeze glue around the edges of the holes to strengthen them (b). Dry.
4. Cut out the flag's designs from different colored fabrics (c).
5. Glue the cutouts to the flag (d). If you wish, you can draw on designs with markers.
6. Tie the flag to the flagpole with cord fed through the holes.
7. Tape the cords to the pole to keep the flag from slipping.

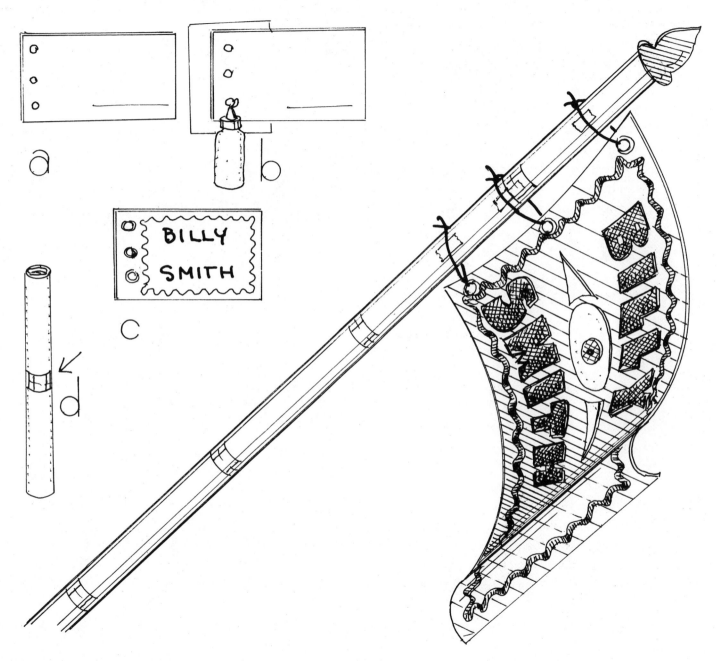

a

b

BILLY
SMITH

c

d

133

African Spear

In many countries in Africa people still use the spear for hunting. It can be thrown long distances to kill animals used for food. The African spear is sometimes used during ceremonies and festivals. This spear will look good standing in a corner of your room or hanging on a wall.

THINGS YOU NEED
paper towel cardboard tubes ★ colored paper
scissors ★ strong tape ★ markers
pencil ★ string

THE SPEAR

1. Cut a triangle from paper for the spear's point (a).
2. Cut two short slits opposite each other in a paper towel tube (b).
3. Slip the spear point into the slits (c).
4. Draw feathers on colored paper. Cut them out.
5. Make a hole at the top of each feather with a sharpened pencil.
6. Tape paper towel tubes together to form a long spear (d). Keep the tube with the spear point at the top.
7. Tie the feathers to the spear with string.

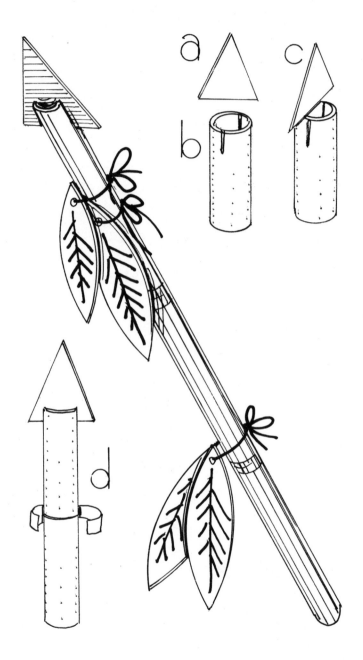

OTHER RECYCLABLES

Drinking Straw Curtain

In some foreign countries rooms are separated by hanging strands of beads. When a person walks through the beads, a wonderful clicking sound fills the air. This drinking straw curtain won't be pleasantly noisy, but it is fun to make. And you can hang it up in your room.

THINGS YOU NEED
drinking straws ★ scissors ★ string ★ cord
beads or small tube macaroni
heavy-duty tape

THE CURTAIN

1. Cut drinking straws into small pieces to make beads (a).
2. Cut lengths of string as long as you want your curtain to be.
3. Tie one end of a length of string to a bead or tube macaroni (b).
4. Add pieces of straw to the string, until you have covered up most of the string (c).
5. Cut a length of cord as wide as you wish the curtain to be (d).
6. Tie the string of straws to one end of the cord (e).
7. Make more strings of straws and tie them to the cord.
8. Have an adult help you hang the curtain inside a doorway with heavy-duty tape.

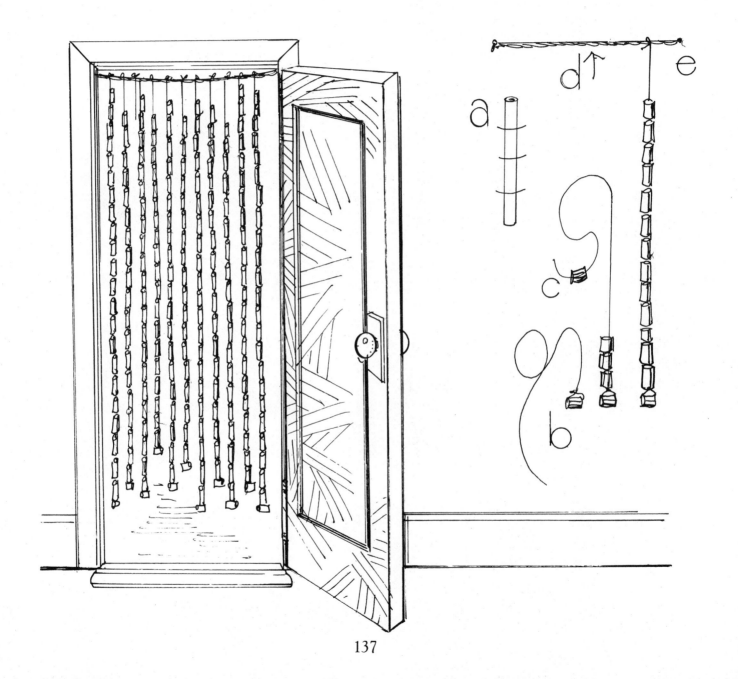

Egg Carton Display Case

You probably have many small favorite things, like pebbles from the beach, a winning marble, a tiny cloth turtle, or a miniature chair. Show off your collection in an egg carton display case. Put it on a desk or hang it on a wall. You could also take it to school to show your classmates and teacher.

THE DISPLAY CASE

1. Cut away the narrow tab at the front of the carton.
2. Squeeze glue into the bottom of the cups of the egg carton. Press a special item into each cup. Heavy things like rocks and marbles will need extra glue. Pins and buttons can be pinned to the sides of the cups.
3. Make two holes into the lid by carefully twisting a sharpened pencil through it. The holes should be near the middle.
4. Cut two lengths of narrow ribbon or yarn a little longer than the carton.
5. Push both ribbons into one hole and out the other.
6. Tie two ribbon ends into a bow.
7. Tie the ends of the other two ribbons into a knot for hanging.

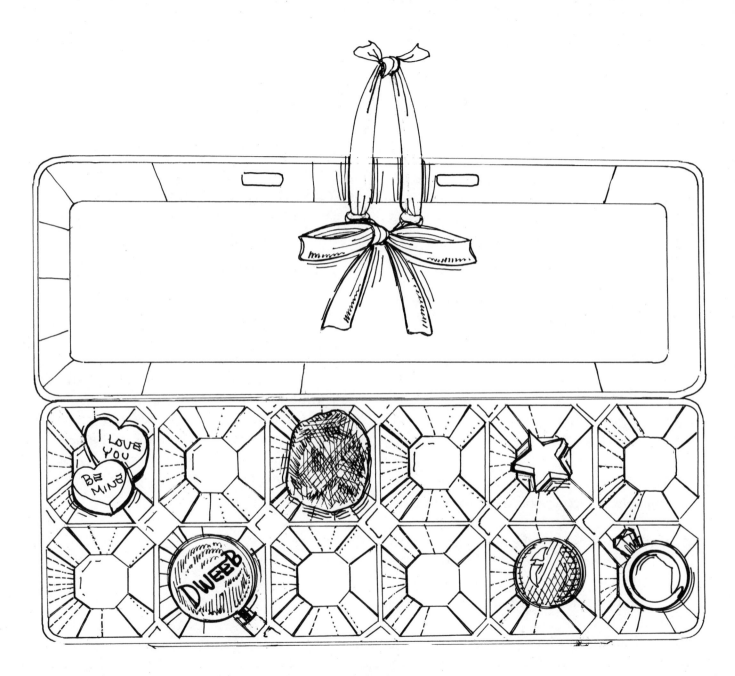

Jar Lid Photo Frames

You know photographs can be put into frames, but how about jar lids? Collect lids of all sizes to make these circular frames. Find or take photographs to fit inside these jar lid frames. Give them to a special adult or friend to hang in the kitchen or to stand on a desk.

Of course, if you don't have photographs, you could draw some pictures of your own to put inside the frames.

THE PHOTO FRAMES

1. Trace the jar lids on paper (a).
2. Cut out circles a little bit smaller than your drawn lines (b).
3. Place the circles on the best part of two photographs. Trace around them with a marker (c).
4. Cut the circles from the photographs. If the photos do not fit inside the lids, trim them a little.
5. Spread paste on the back of each photograph (d).
6. Press each photo into a lid (e).
7. Cut a ribbon shape with a point from colored paper. Also cut out a bow.
8. Paste the bow to the straight end of the ribbon. Tape string to the back of the bow (f).
9. Glue the lids to the ribbon.
10. For standing frames, cut a triangle from cardboard. Fold back the top and glue it to the back of the lid (see the arrow in g). Stand the frame (h).

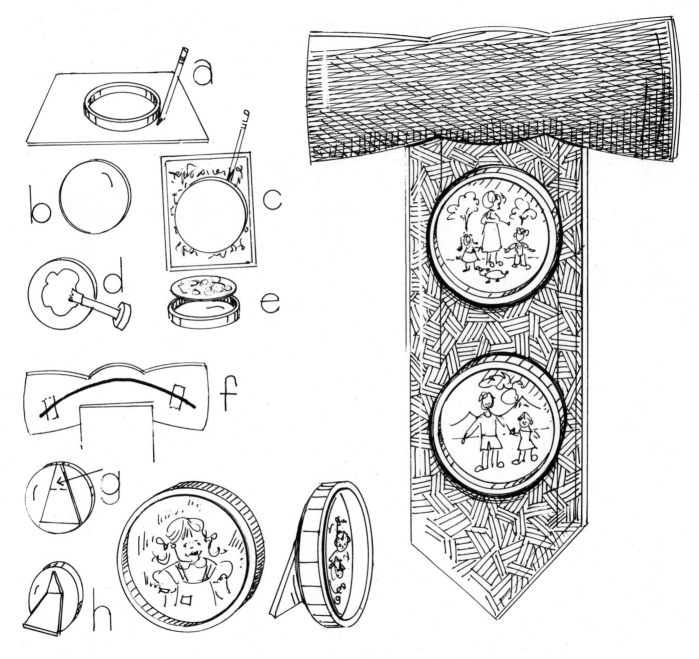

Junk Mail Beads

Junk mail includes all those unwanted catalogs and advertisements that are mailed to your home. Instead of throwing them into the wastebasket or recycled paper bin, save the most colorful ones for this project.

Make dozens and dozens of paper beads. Design a jewel box full of necklaces, bracelets, and other beaded treasures.

THE NECKLACE

1. Cut a long triangle from cardboard (the same size as the one shown in a) for the pattern.
2. Use the pattern to trace triangles on the colored photographs or brightly colored parts of junk mail and catalogs.
3. Place a triangle on waxed paper with the good side facing down. Spread paste over the entire back.
4. Wrap the pasted short end of a triangle around the top of the straw (b).
5. Continue to wrap the paper around itself. Add extra paste to the tip before finishing the wrapping (c).

THINGS YOU NEED
junk mail and catalogs ★ cardboard ★ pencil
scissors ★ waxed paper ★ paste
cord thin enough to fit into a straw

6. Cut away the bead from the straw (d).
7. Make dozens of beads.
8. String the beads on cord. You can add a round paper charm to the necklace, if you wish.

142

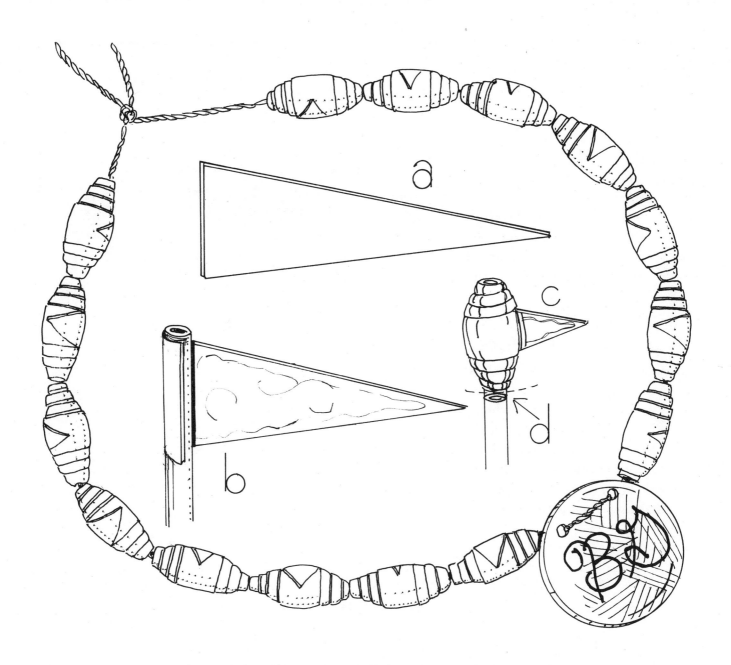

a

b

c

d

143

Meat Tray Steaks & Chops

Pretend you are a butcher and you are filling up your meat cases. You will need some beefsteaks, some lamb chops, some bacon, and some ham slices. If you go shopping with your parents, then you know what these meats look like. You can also package fish and chicken parts.

THE STEAKS AND CHOPS

1. Draw a meat shape on corrugated cardboard (a). It should fit inside a tray. Cut it out.
2. Cut a bone or fat from white paper.
3. Paste the bone to the meat (b).
4. Place the meat on a clean meat tray.
5. Lay cellophane wrap over the tray (c).
6. Fold the sides of the wrap onto the back of the tray. Tape them in place (d).

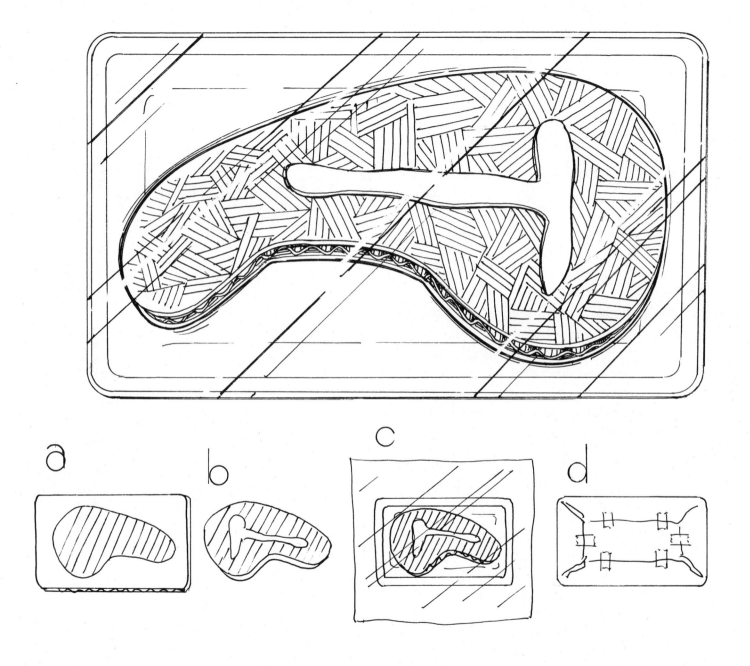

Newspaper Fern

A newspaper fern is a magical plant. With just four cuts—presto—the floppiest fern you will ever see pulls out of rolled newspapers. For a really tall fern, use a lot of newspapers.

THE FERN

1. Loosely roll an opened sheet of newspaper up to the fold mark, starting at a short side (a).
2. Place half of a second sheet onto the unrolled half of the first sheet (b).
3. Again roll to the fold.
4. Continue adding and rolling sheets of newspaper as you did the first two. Use at least five sheets.
5. Tape the last sheet in place (c).
6. Cut four slits into one end of the rolled papers (d). They should be halfway down and evenly spaced.
7. To make the fern, stick your fingers into the cut end and slowly pull the fern leaves up and out (e).

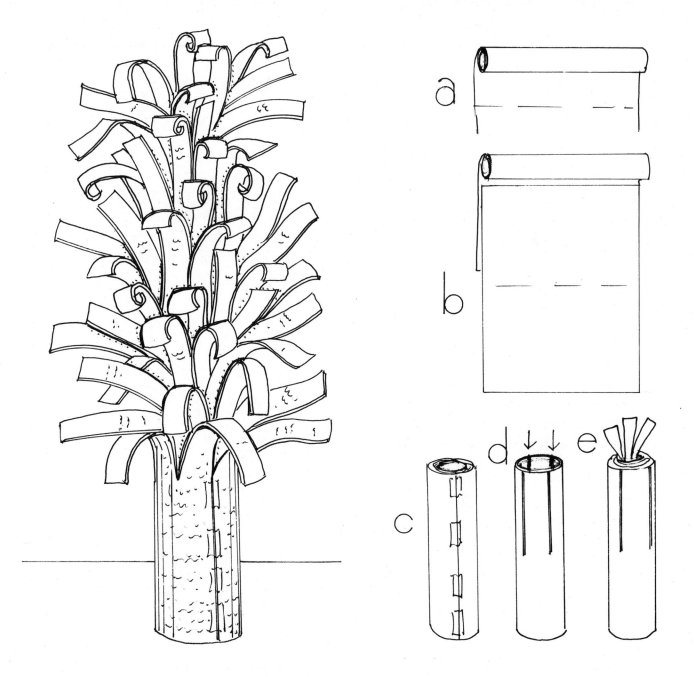

Plastic Flatware Sunburst

This sunburst has plastic spoons and forks shooting out in all directions instead of sunrays. This fancy sun makes a sunny wall hanging in your room or on your bedroom door.

THE SUNBURST

1. Draw a sunny face on the inside of the plate with crayons or markers (a).
2. Make two holes in the side of the plate above the face.
3. Feed cord into the holes (b). Knot the ends.
4. Turn the plate over.
5. Glue the handles of plastic spoons and forks to the underside of the plate (c). Use lots of glue.
6. Hang when dry.

THINGS YOU NEED
yellow or white paper or foam plate
yellow or white plastic spoons and forks
cord ★ white glue ★ crayons or markers
pencil

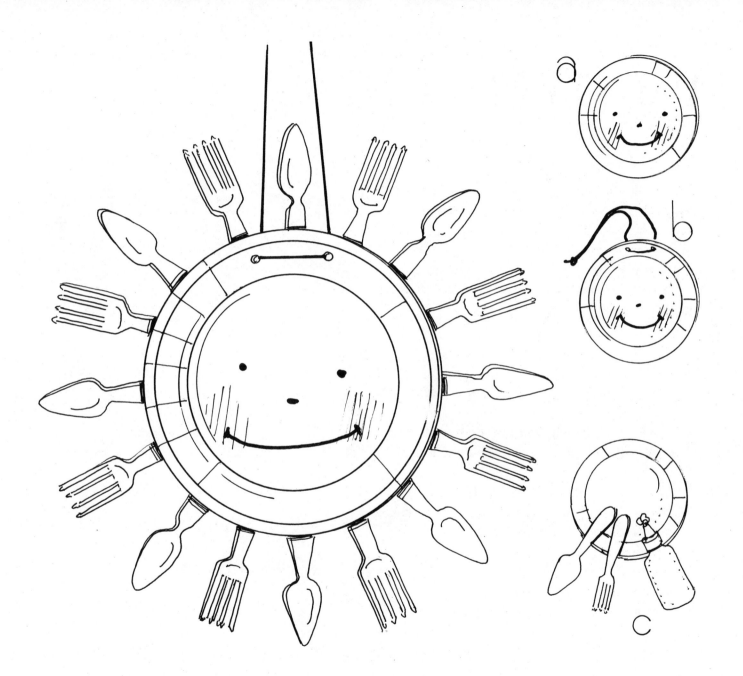

Pie Tin Plaster Cast

Here's a pie that will be as hard as cement but as pretty as a picture. This pie is not for eating! The recipe is simple. The pie's filling is plaster. The top decorations are dried beans, lentils, and other small things you choose. After the plaster mixture has set, remove the plaster cast, and find a special place for your pie.

THE PIE

1. Spread butter on the bottom and sides of a pie tin (a).
2. Have an adult help you mix plaster of Paris in a can according to package directions.
3. Spoon the wet plaster into the pie tin (b).
4. Quickly push things into the plaster (c). You can make a flower design with beans and lentils (shown in the drawing), or use your imagination.
5. When the plaster has hardened, turn the tin upside down on a sheet of paper. Remove the pie tin (d). Turn your plaster pie right side up.

151

Bottle Cap
Toss Game

Do you have a good aim? If you do, then see how well you can play this toss game. You will need a small collection of bottle caps of different sizes and small things, like dried beans or pennies, to toss into them. You can write numbers on the caps to tell you how many points each player gets if a penny or bean lands in it. Or you can leave your caps plain, and the person who gets the most beans or pennies inside the caps wins.

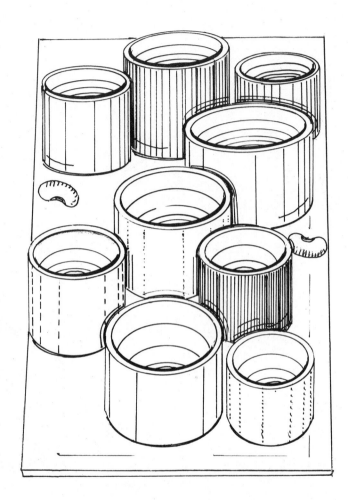

THINGS YOU NEED
many different size bottle caps ★ cardboard
white glue ★ dried beans or pennies

THE GAME

1. Glue a collection of different sizes of bottle caps close together on a piece of cardboard.
2. To play the game, each player gets ten beans or pennies. The player stands a certain distance from the caps and tosses the beans or pennies into the caps.

CELEBRATIONS

Birthday Cakes

The calendar is filled with the birth dates of many famous people. Honor your favorite heroes by making and decorating this special cake. Have a birthday celebration every month. And don't forget to include the most important birthday of all—yours.

THE CAKE

1. Tape the open end of a box closed. The box can be round, square, rectangular or any shape you can find.
2. Trace the top and four sides of the box on colored paper (a). Cut them out.
3. Write HAPPY BIRTHDAY and draw cake icing designs on the top paper cutout. Draw cake icing designs on the side cutouts.
4. Glue the top and sides to the box to form the cake (b).
5. Cut colored paper as tall as a tube and long enough to wrap around it (c).
6. Tape the paper in place to form the candle (d).
7. Cut a flame from colored paper.
8. Paste the flame into the top of the candle.
9. Stand the candle on top of the cake.

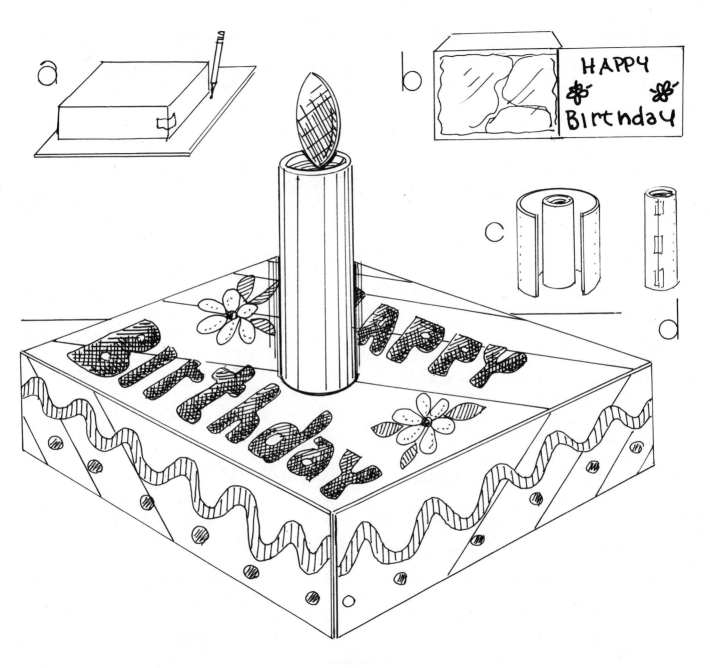

Pin the Nose on the Clowns

Here's a party game that you have five chances to win. The target is a circus of clown faces. The object of the game is to pin a red, round nose on one of them. It may sound easy, but don't forget, you and your friends will be blindfolded. Whoever comes closest to a bull's-eye is the winner. This game is fun at a birthday party or almost any kind of party.

THE CLOWN BOARD

1. Tape a small length of cord to a sheet of poster board at the top (a).
2. Turn the board over. The side with the cord is at the top.
3. Squeeze glue on the top rim of a plate (b).
4. Place the glued plate on the middle of the board (c).
5. Glue the other plates to the board around the first plate (d).
6. Cut out two eyes, two cheeks, and a mouth from colored paper for each clown face. Also cut out a hat for each top clown face, hair for the middle face, and a collar and bow tie for the bottom faces.

THINGS YOU NEED
sheet of poster board ★ five paper plates colored paper ★ scissors ★ white glue cord ★ tape ★ paste ★ crayons or markers

7. Paste your cutouts on the plates.
8. Draw an X on each plate where the nose should be.
9. Draw a colorful border around the board with crayons or markers.
10. Cut circles from red paper for the clowns' noses.

TO PLAY THE GAME

1. Hang the board on the wall.
2. Take turns. Blindfold each player and give him or her a nose with a piece of tape attached to it.
3. Spin each player around and direct him or her toward the clown board.
4. The player who tapes his or her nose closest to an X is the winner.

a

b

c

d

157

Valentine's Day Heart

Valentine's Day is the holiday when you give a token of your love to someone special. On this day we remember how the winged Cupid shoots his arrows of love. Give this heart with an arrow and a pretty bow to your mom, dad, sister, brother, favorite aunt, grandma, or to another special someone.

THE HEART

1. Cut a scalloped design around the edge of a paper plate (a).
2. Cut a heart larger than the plate from red paper.
3. With a sharpened pencil make two holes in the center of the heart and the plate (b).
4. Feed the ends of a long ribbon or piece of yarn through the holes in the heart. Then feed the ribbon or yarn through the holes in the plate (c).
5. Tie the ribbon into a bow.
6. Cut out an arrow from black paper. Paste it to the back of the heart.
7. Write a Valentine's Day message on the plate with crayons or markers.

THINGS YOU NEED
white paper plate ★ red and black paper
pencil ★ narrow ribbon or yarn ★ paste
crayons or markers ★ scissors

St. Patrick's Day Leprechauns

Leprechauns are mischievous fairies in Irish folk-lore who look like little old people. They are very tiny and difficult to see. They live in the forests of Ireland. And some people say that these fairies know where to find buried treasure.

The luck of the Irish must be with you. Here are two smiling leprechauns looking for a home. They don't go around playing silly tricks. Mr. and Ms. Leprechaun carry special good-luck shamrocks, just for you.

THE LEPRECHAUNS

1. Wrap green paper around two paper cups. Tape in place (a).
2. Trim the paper away from the bottom and the top of each cup (see the dotted lines in a).
3. For each cup, cut two arms from green paper. Glue on skin-colored hands.
4. Paste two arms to the back of each cup (b).
5. Draw Mr. and Ms. Leprechaun's faces on skin-colored paper. Cut them out.
6. Glue gathered yarn hair to the top of each head (c). Glue a hat to Mr. Leprechaun's hair.

THINGS YOU NEED
paper cups ★ colored paper ★ scissors ★ tape paste ★ crayons or markers ★ yarn white glue

7. Glue the faces to the cups (d).
8. Cut an apron, belt, bow tie, shamrocks, and a pipe from colored paper.
9. Paste the cutouts to Mr. and Ms. Leprechaun, as shown in the drawing.

a

b

c

d

e

Arbor Day Tree

Julius Sterling Morton thought it would be a good idea to have a holiday for trees. He called it Arbor Day. He knew what the world would look like if trees were cut down and not replanted. He also knew that trees were important for building everything from houses to boats. On this special day, people plant trees so that the Earth will remain green and beautiful in the future.

Here's a little apple tree that you can make to honor this day. Maybe you and your friends can also go outside and plant a real little tree.

THE APPLE TREE

1. Tape three cans together (a).
2. From a brown paper grocery bag, cut paper that is as tall as the taped cans and long enough to wrap around them (b).
3. Tape the paper in place (c).
4. Fill a sandwich bag firmly with crumpled newspaper (d).
5. Fit the bottom of the bag over the top of the cans. Tie the bag tightly in place with cord (e).
6. Draw leaves on green paper and apples on red paper (f). Cut out the leaves and apples.
7. Paste the leaves and apples on the paper bag (g). Cover it completely.

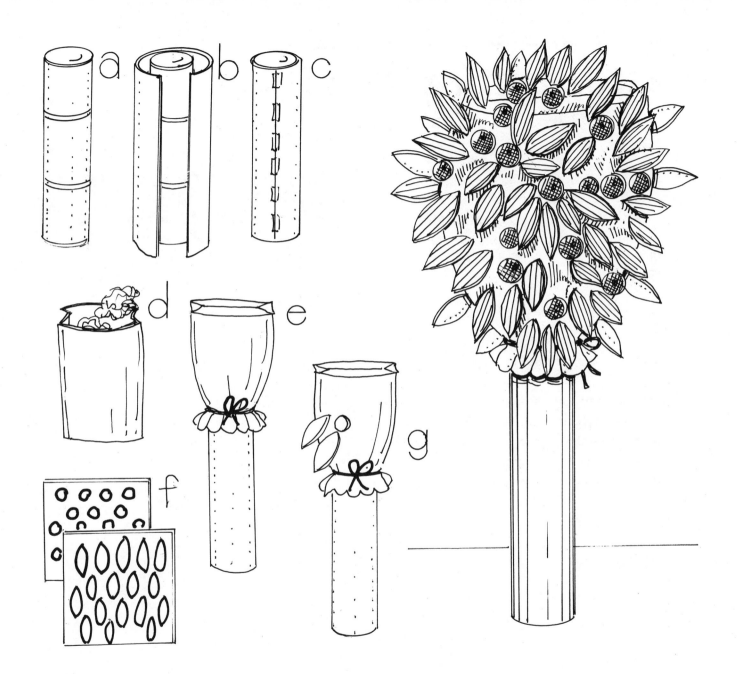

Easter Bunny Family

"Here comes Peter Cottontail, hopping down the bunny trail . . ." You probably know the rest of the words of this popular song. Mr., Mrs., and Baby Bunny are the new rabbits on the block. Give them special names and make up a song about them this Easter.

THINGS YOU NEED
one large, one medium, and one small can
white and colored paper ★ scissors ★ tape
pencil ★ paste ★ crayons or markers

THE EASTER BUNNIES

1. Cut white paper as tall as each can and long enough to wrap around it. Tape each in place (a).
2. Trace around the bottom of each can on white paper. Cut the circles out (b).
3. Paste the circles to the tops of the cans (c).
4. Draw two ears on white paper for each bunny. Color inner ears pink.
5. Paste the ears to the tops of the cans (d).
6. Cut out a pink nose and two cheeks for each bunny.
7. Paste the noses and cheeks in place (d). Draw on eyes, whiskers, and mouths.
8. Paste a paper bow tie on Papa and Baby Bunny and a collar and flower on Mama Bunny.

Halloween Pumpkins

Here are four happy pumpkins to add to your trick-or-treat fun. You can also make blown egg (e) and paper plate (f) pumpkins.

THE TIN CAN PUMPKIN (A)

1. Cut orange paper as tall as a tin can or round box and long enough to wrap around it. Tape in place.
2. Trace the bottom of the can on orange paper. Cut out the paper and glue it to the top.
3. Paste on a black paper face or draw on a face with a black marker.
4. Glue on a bottle cap for the stem.

THE JAR PUMPKIN (B)

1. Paint the inside of a jar with orange paint.
2. Paste a black paper face on the jar or draw a face with a black marker.
3. Glue on a bottle cap for the stem.

THE BOX PUMPKIN (C)

1. Trace the sides and top of a box on orange paper. Cut them out.
2. Paste the cutouts on the box.

THINGS YOU NEED
tin can or round container ★ jar
box ★ brown paper grocery bag
markers or crayons ★ poster paints
white glue ★ colored paper ★ food coloring
bottle caps ★ drinking straw ★ paste
bathroom tissue cardboard tube
newspaper ★ paintbrush

3. Paste on a black paper face or draw on a face with a black marker.
4. Glue on a green paper stem.

THE PAPER BAG PUMPKIN (D)

1. Half fill a brown paper grocery bag with crumpled newspaper.
2. Cut into the four folded edges of the open half of the bag (see Totem Pole on page 14).
3. Fold over the sides. Tape them in place.
4. Paste on a black paper face, or draw on a face with a black marker.
5. Glue on a toilet paper cardboard tube painted green for the stem.

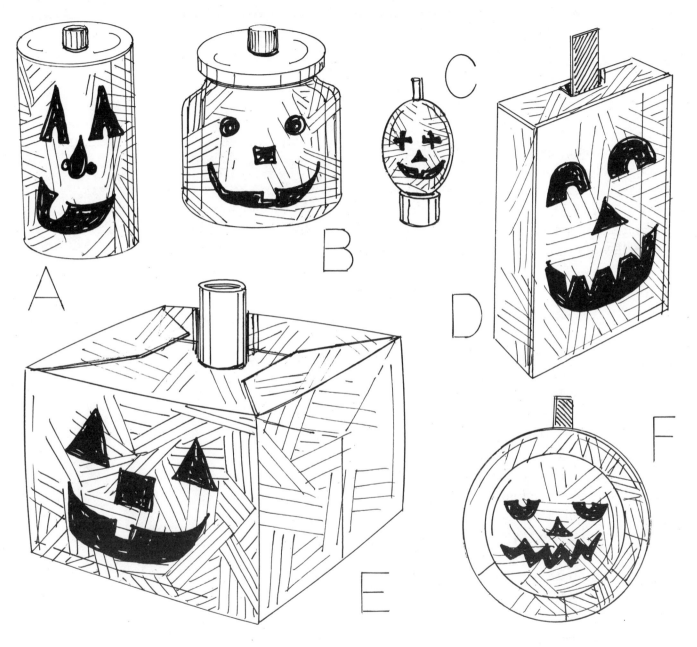

A

B

C

D

E

F

167

Halloween Witch

Who wears a long, pointy black hat, a long black dress, and flies around on a broom? The Allhallows Eve witch, that's who. This witch may look mean and grumpy but deep down she's a tame pussycat. Remember that you have the power this Halloween to make her smile.

THINGS YOU NEED
small paper cup ★ colored paper ★ tape paste ★ blown egg ★ crayons or markers white glue ★ bottle cap ★ scissors

THE WITCH

1. Roll black paper around a paper cup. Tape in place (a).
2. Trim away the paper at the top and bottom of the cup (see the dotted lines in a).
3. Cut out the bottom of the cup (b).
4. Cut two arms from black paper. Glue them to the back of the cup (c).
5. Draw a witch's face on a blown egg.
6. Cut a strip from black paper for the hair. Cut slits into one long side.
7. Paste the hair around the top of the egg (d).
8. Rest the egg on the cutout end of the cup (e).
9. For the witch's hat, roll black paper into a cone and tape it in place. Trim the bottom to fit on the head.
10. Paste a paper broom to a hand.
11. Make another witch's head and rest it on a bottle cap.

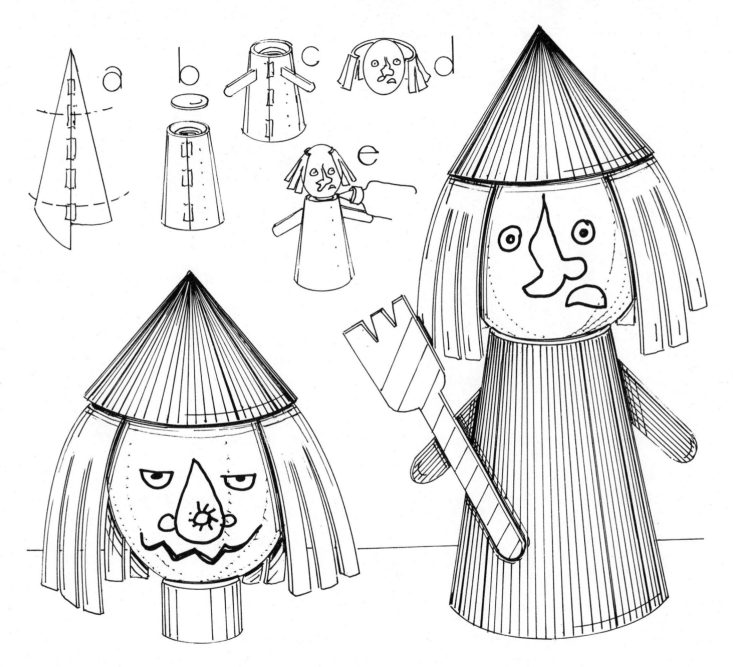

Chanukah Dreidel

Chanukah is the Festival of Lights in Jewish tradition. This holiday celebrates the rededication of the Temple in Jerusalem. More than 2,000 years ago, an oil lamp in the temple burned for eight days on just a one-day supply of oil. That is why a candle or an oil lamp is lit on each of the eight days of Chanukah. During this holiday children spin the dreidel for small coins. You can make your own dreidel and play this game.

THE DREIDEL

1. Draw a line around a carton with a crayon (see the dotted lines in a). The bottom half should be a square.
2. Cut away the peak and three sides of the carton up to the drawn line. You will be left with a box with a long lid (a).
3. Fold the lid over the open end of the box. Tape the lid in place (b).
4. Trace the bottom of the box on white paper (c). Cut out and paste on the lid.
5. Trace a side of the box four times. Cut the paper sides out.
6. Draw one letter of the Hebrew alphabet on each cutout (see letters 1 to 4).

7. Paste the sides to the box (d).
8. Draw lines, from corner to corner, on the top and bottom of the box (e).
9. Make a hole where each two lines cross by carefully twisting a sharpened pencil back and forth (study e).
10. Push the worn point of a pencil through the top hole and out the bottom hole (f). The point should extend out a little.
11. To play the game, each player gets the same number of pennies. Each player then puts one penny in the pot. The first player spins the dreidel. If it lands on the letter *Nun* (1), the player gets nothing; the letter *Shin* (2), the player has to put one penny in the pot; the letter *Hay* (3), the player takes half of the pennies; and the letter *Gimel* (4), the player takes all the pennies. Add a penny with each new spin.

a

b

c

d

e

f

1.

2.

3.

4.

Christmas Wreath

A wreath made of winter greenery and hung on a door is a popular Christmas decoration. Here's a wreath that's easy to make and as traditional as the holiday itself. This wreath is made up of green holly leaves, red holly berries, and a big red bow. Hang this one on your front door to welcome holiday visitors.

Other wreaths made with dried plants and flowers are popular year round. You could make look-alikes out of paper.

THE WREATH

1. Place a plate on a table with the underside facing up.
2. Draw a circle on the plate that is smaller than the bottom. Use a compass or trace around a small round dish or a mug.
3. Cut out the drawn circle (see shaded area in a). This forms a ring.
4. Draw holly leaves on white or green paper (b).
5. Cut out the holly leaves.
6. Tie some string to the ring (c).

THINGS YOU NEED
paper plate ★ compass ★ scissors ★ red paper green paper ★ string ★ paste

7. Paste leaves on the ring (d). They should overlap each other a little. Cover the entire ring with leaves to form the wreath.
8. Cut out a bow and round holly berries from red paper (e).
9. Paste the berries on the leaves.
10. Paste the bow on the wreath.
11. Hang the wreath by the string on a door or in another special place.

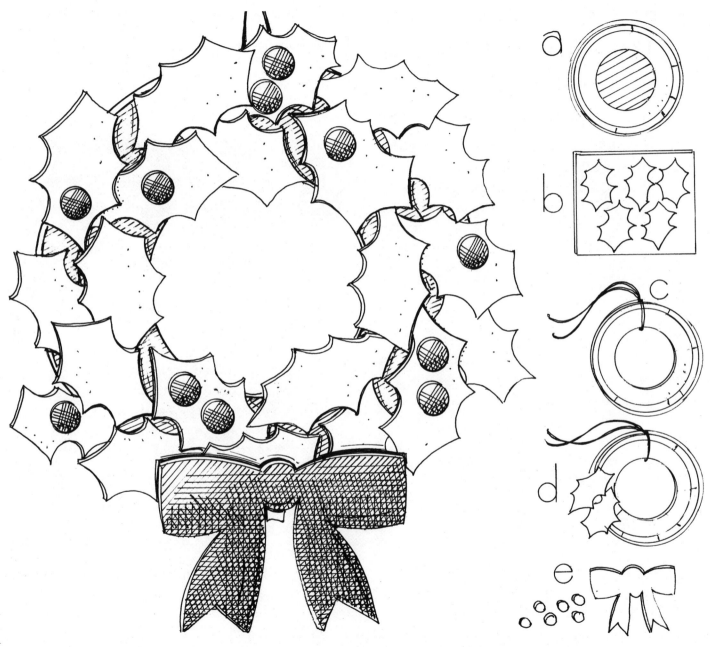

Christmas Tree Ornaments

The first Christmas tree ornaments were hand-made. They were paper cones filled with candies, paper flags, and angels made of cotton and tinsel. Blown eggs have many uses. Here are some "eggs-traordinary" decorations to hang on your tree. Make your own angel, Santa Claus or Father Christmas, and Rudolph the Red-Nosed Reindeer ornaments.

FOR EACH EGG

1. Dye a blown egg in food coloring or egg dyes, or use the egg as is.
2. Add a button to a length of string. Knot the ends together.
3. Stand the egg on a bottle cap.
4. Squeeze glue on top of the egg (a).
5. Press the button onto the glue (b).

THE ANGEL (A)

1. Draw a face and hair on an egg.
2. Cut wings from white paper. Draw on feathers.
3. Glue the wings to the back of the egg.

SANTA CLAUS (FATHER CHRISTMAS) (B)

1. Draw Santa's face on an egg.
2. Glue a cotton ball beard on the egg.
3. Glue on a paper moustache.
4. Roll red paper into a small cone. Cut away a little bit of the tip. Trim the bottom edge.
5. Feed the string through the hat and rest it on Santa's head.

THE RED-NOSED REINDEER (C)

1. Draw Rudolph's face on an egg. Be sure to make his nose red.
2. Draw two antlers on brown paper. Cut them out.
3. Glue the antlers to the back of the egg.

New Year's Eve Father Time

Father Time represents the old year that ends on New Year's Eve, December 31st, just before January 1st. He is an old man with a long white beard who holds a scythe in one hand and an hourglass in another. An hourglass is an old-fashioned clock. On New Year's Eve we watch the clock and wait until midnight. That's when we say good-bye to the old year with lots of noise and revelry.

It gets noisy at midnight all over Earth. That's because most people use the Gregorian calendar with 365 days for a year, plus an extra day every leap year. But traditional Jewish, Muslim, Chinese, and other new years begin at different times.

On New Year's Eve, let Father Time help you welcome the baby new year. Bang a pot, blow a horn, toss some confetti, and shout as loudly as you can, "Happy New Year!"

FATHER TIME

1. Cut white paper as tall as a tube and long enough to wrap around it.
2. Tape the paper to the tube.
3. Place the tube on white paper and trace

around the bottom (a). Cut out.
4. Squeeze glue around the edge of the circle (b).
5. Place the glued circle on the end of the tube (c).
6. Draw a face at the top of the tube (d).
7. Cut a long beard from white fabric. The top of the fabric should wrap around the tube.
8. Glue the top of the beard to the tube under the face (e).
9. Cut two arms from white paper.
10. Glue the arms to the back of the tube.
11. Draw an hourglass and a scythe blade on colored paper (g). Cut them out.
12. Glue the scythe blade to the top of a drinking straw.
13. Tape the scythe and hourglass to Father Time's hands.

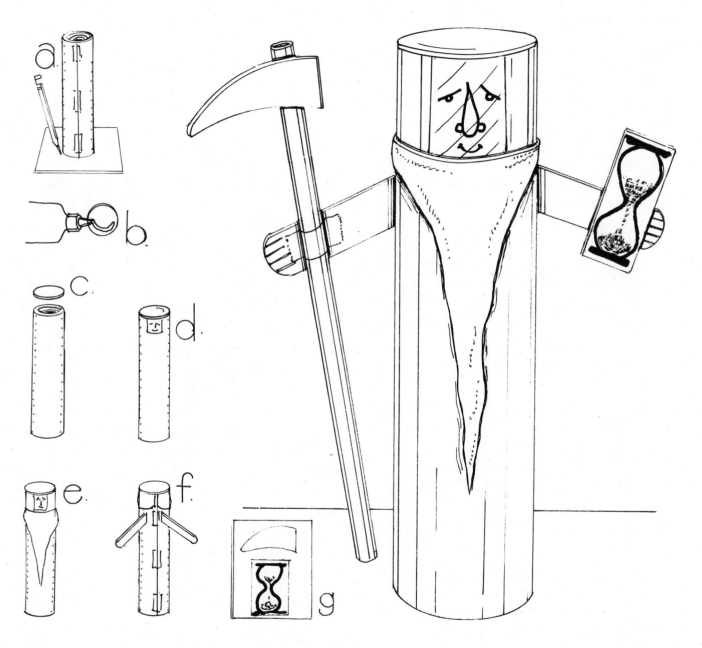

Earth Day

Earth Day is an international holiday that celebrates the water, the land, and the sky. It is the day to think about the wonders of nature and how we can keep them wondrous forever. Recycling is one thing we all can do to keep flowers growing in the ground, fish swimming in the seas, and birds flying in the sky.

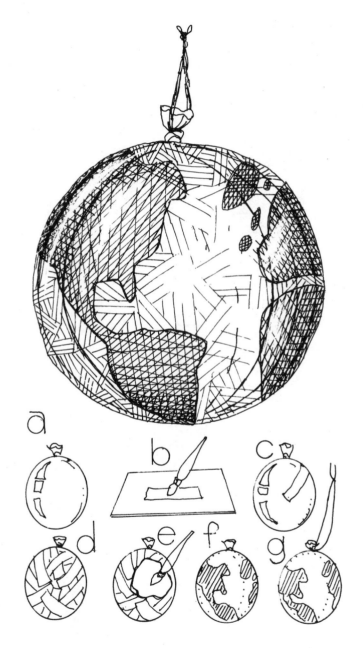

THINGS YOU NEED
round balloon ★ newspaper ★ waxed paper poster paints ★ paintbrush ★ string ★ paste

THE EARTH

1. Blow up a round balloon. Knot the neck (a).
2. Rip newspaper into short, narrow strips.
3. Place a strip of newspaper on a sheet of waxed paper. Spread paste on the top side of the strip (b).
4. Lay the strip on the balloon (c).
5. Paste more newspaper strips and lay them on the balloon. They should overlap each other a little. Cover the entire balloon twice (d).
6. Paint the dry balloon with white paint (e).
7. Paint the balloon light blue for the oceans. Paint the continents brown (f). Check an atlas at the library.
8. Tie string to the neck (g). Hang.

KNOW YOUR EARTH QUIZ SHOW

Mother Earth, the Moderator

Mother Earth is billions of years old. She is round and mostly blue. Her one satellite, whom we call Moon, follows her on her journey every year around the Sun. For the most part, she has been happy with all her children—animals, fish, birds, and people. But lately, she has been saddened by the way that people have been mistreating her.

Mother Earth has agreed to be the moderator of the Know Your Earth Quiz Show. She has prepared many questions for her panelists and for us to think about.

MOTHER EARTH AND MOON

1. Choose a blue plate for Mother Earth. If you only have a white plate, color the underside blue with a marker, crayon, or poster paint.
2. Draw on brown paper North and South America, or Europe and Africa, or Asia and Australia. If you live on an island, like Hawaii, Puerto Rico, or New Zealand, be sure to draw it, too. Study an atlas or globe for their shapes.
3. Cut out the continents from colored paper. Paste them to the underside of the plate.

THINGS YOU NEED
blue or white plate ★ colored paper crayons or markers ★ poster paints ★ scissors paste ★ pipe cleaner ★ paper punch paintbrush ★ cord

4. Draw Mother Earth's eyes and mouth with crayons or markers.
5. Draw a small round Moon on colored paper. Cut it out. Draw Moon's eyes and mouth with crayons or markers.
6. Tape Moon to one end of a pipe cleaner (a).
7. Tape the other end of the pipe cleaner to the back of Mother Earth (b).
8. Make two holes at the top of Mother Earth (c). Use a paper punch or carefully twist a sharpened pencil through the plate.
9. Feed a long cord or some yarn through the hole (c).

181

Al U. Minium, Tin Tin Tin, & Claire Glass, the Panelists

Three panelists have been selected to appear on the Know Your Earth Quiz Show. They will try to answer Mother Earth's questions.

Al U. Minium is a member of the Element family. He is shiny and lightweight. And he can live a long, long life in many different shapes.

Tin Tin Tin, the faithful *can*ine, also belongs to the Element family. If he stays out in the rain long enough, he will rust away.

Claire Glass was born from melted sand. Since she has a see-through personality, she has nothing to hide.

AL U. MINIUM (A)

1. Cut a piece of paper as tall as an aluminum can and long enough to wrap around it. Tape it in place.
2. With the open end at the bottom, draw Al U. Minium's face on the paper.
3. Draw two ears on colored paper. Cut them out.
4. Fold back part of each ear. Paste the folded parts to the can.

THINGS YOU NEED
aluminum can ★ small tin can
glass jar with lid ★ white and colored paper
scissors ★ tape ★ cord ★ crayons or markers
paste ★ paper clips

TIN TIN TIN (B)

1. Remove the label from a tin can. If the can has printing on it, cover the can with colored paper.
2. With the open end at the bottom, draw Tin Tin Tin's face on the can with crayons.
3. Cut out two ears. Paste them to the can.

CLAIRE GLASS

1. Remove the label from a jar with warm water.
2. Draw on Claire Glass's face with crayons.
3. Paste a piece of paper with cut slits on the side of the lid for hair.

A

B

C

183

Television Set

Turn the television on to the recycling channel. Mother Earth chats with today's panelists before the show begins. Once the program begins, there will be no commercial interruptions.

THE TELEVISION

1. Draw a television screen on the long side of a carton (see arrow in a).
2. Ask an adult to help you cut out the screen. Also cut away the top of the carton (see shaded areas in a).
3. Paint the carton with poster paint if it has printing on it.
4. Paste on round paper knobs.
5. Paste colored paper or gift wrap paper to the inside of the carton.
6. Cut two long bars from the cutaway cardboard. Lay them across the open carton's top.
7. Cover a cereal box with paper to make a platform for the panelists. Place it inside the television on an angle.

ADDING PULL CORDS

1. Ask an adult to make a hole in the top of Al U. Minium and Tin Tin Tin. Also make a

hole in Claire Glass's lid. The holes should be centered.
2. Push a long cord through each hole (c). The cords should go completely through the cans.
3. Tie a paper clip to the end of each cord (d). Pull the cords until the paper clips rest against the holes.
4. Twist the lid onto Claire Glass (e).

HOW TO SET THE STAGE

1. Stand the panelists on the cereal box inside the television. Tie their cords to a bar.
2. Tie Mother Earth to the other bar. She should hang off the floor.
3. When each character speaks, tug on his or her cord just enough to make him or her move a little.

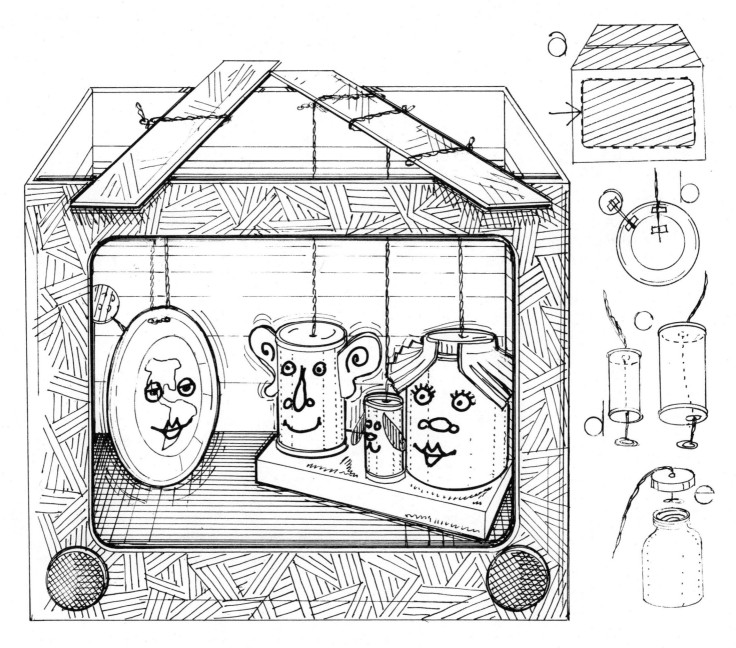

Know Your Earth Quiz Show

Here are a few helpful hints for you and your stage crew to make this television program about Mother Earth a success.

BEFORE THE SHOW

1. Select a stage crew to help make the quiz show a success. You can have as many as five stagehands helping backstage on the day of the production. Each stagehand will help one of the performers—Mother Earth, Moon, Al U. Minium, Claire Glass, and Tin Tin Tin. If the television set is small, two stagehands will work best. Then each stagehand will help more than one performer.

2. Make a photocopy of the script for each stagehand who will speak for a character. A younger player can say Moon's lines or invent new cheers for Mother Earth.

3. Have several rehearsals before the show. Each stagehand should develop a voice for the character or characters he or she helps.

4. Hand out invitations announcing the première of the Know Your Earth Quiz Show a week ahead.

5. Plan what refreshments you will offer your audience. Peanuts, popcorn, fruit snacks, and juices are healthy choices.

THE DAY OF THE SHOW

1. Choose a small room, like your bedroom or family room, for the viewing.

2. Place the television on a table, with the screen facing the audience. Place the table near a wall or in a corner of the room. You can also place the table in a doorway.

3. Ask an adult to string a rope from wall to wall or across the top of the doorway. Drape a sheet over the rope. The bottom of the sheet should fall on the top of the television. This will separate the stage crew from the audience.

4. Set up chairs in front of the television or scatter pillows on the floor.

5. To make the television look like it is turned off, place a piece of poster board, cut larger than the open screen, inside the box.

6. When the performance begins, remove the poster board in front of the screen.

7. Shine a flashlight (torch) on the performers when they are speaking. That will look like a spotlight. Remember to jiggle the string of each performer when he or she speaks.

8. After the performance, have the characters ask the audience for any questions. Then, it

will be fun to exchange ideas about the environment and how everyone can help protect it.

9. After the audience leaves, sweep up the crumbs, and collect the paper plates and cups.

10. If any refreshments came in recyclable containers, remember to save them for future projects.

KNOW YOUR EARTH Quiz Show

Moderator MOTHER EARTH with MOON

Panelists AL U. MINIUM

CLAIRE GLASS

TIN TIN TIN

(Remove the poster board screen cover on your TV set.)

MOTHER EARTH *(in a soft, kind voice)*
I would like to welcome you, children of the Earth, to the Know Your Earth Quiz Show. I am Mother Earth. Floating above me is Moon. Moon follows me wherever I go around the heavens.

MOON *(very excited, in a high-pitched voice)*
Let's hear it for Mother Earth!

(Stage crew claps, to encourage audience applause, every time Moon cheers Mother Earth.)

MOTHER EARTH
Thank you for caring about me and my beautiful rivers, oceans, mountains, and plains. Today we are going to quiz some experts on how well they know me.

MOON
Let's hear it for Mother Earth!

MOTHER EARTH
Now I would like to introduce the panel. First is Mr. Al U. Minium who is a member of the Element family. He appears frequently in groceries and is very popular with the thirsty crowd. Al, would you tell us something about yourself?

AL U. MINIUM *(in a goofy voice)*
Sure can. *(He laughs.)* Get it? Can?

MOTHER EARTH *(with patience)*
Yes, Al, we get it. Would you please continue.

AL U. MINIUM
I am made of the metal that soft drinks and other beverages come in. I am popular because aluminum is a plentiful metal and it is lightweight, too. I am a very shiny guy.

MOTHER EARTH
Thank you very much, Al. Next, I would like to introduce Claire Glass. Claire is also a popular personality in groceries. She has many fans, including those who love pickles, applesauce, and beets.

AL U. MINIUM
Beets! Yuk!

MOTHER EARTH
Now, now, Al, you had your turn. And there are many people who like my ruby red beets. Claire, would you please introduce yourself?

CLAIRE GLASS (*in a bouncy voice*)
Well, my mother is beach sand and my father is the hot heat of fire. When they met, I was born. But I don't look anything like them. People like me because I have a see-through personality. I'm simply transparent!

MOTHER EARTH
Thank you, Claire. Lastly, I want to introduce Tin Tin Tin. Like Al, he belongs to the Element family. He is made of the most popular metal found on grocery shelves. Tin, would you tell us about yourself?

TIN TIN TIN
Bow wow, ruff, ruff, bow wow, woof, woof, woof!

MOTHER EARTH
Thank you, Tin. Would everyone give our panelists a round of applause.

(*Stage crew claps to encourage applause.*)

MOTHER EARTH
The first question of today's quiz is about the ozone layer. Can anyone tell me where it is?

AL U. MINIUM (*jumps up and down excitedly*)
It's between the *N* Zone and the *P* Zone.

MOTHER EARTH (*stresses the words*)
Not *0* Zone. **Ozone.** The **ozone layer** is high in the atmosphere that is all around me. It protects my children from getting a serious sunburn from the ultraviolet rays of the sun. Does anyone know what is happening to the ozone layer?

TIN TIN TIN
Woof, woof, bow, wow, wow.

MOTHER EARTH
No, Tin, it's not turning a really deep purple. What has happened is that my children have been creating many harmful gases that rise into my sky and make holes in the ozone layer. Some gases can really hurt the ozone layer.

MOON
Let's hear it for Mother Earth!

MOTHER EARTH
The next question is about **air pollution.** Can anyone tell me what it is?

CLAIRE GLASS
I know what it is. Air pollution is gossip. People open their mouths and gibber-gabber fills the air.

MOTHER EARTH

No, Claire, that's not right. **Air pollution** comes from all the harmful chemicals rising into my cool, crisp air, from cars, factories, and spray cans.

TIN TIN TIN

Woof, woof, ruff, ruff, bow, wow, ruff.

MOTHER EARTH

Yes, Tin, like the hair spray in a can you use on your floppy ears. Unless we stop polluting the air, I am afraid I will become very unhappy and unhealthy in the future. **My environment** will not be healthy for my plants and my children.

MOON

Let's hear it for Mother Earth!

MOTHER EARTH

The next question is connected to air pollution. What is the **greenhouse effect?**

AL U. MINIUM

It's when you paint your white house green.

MOTHER EARTH (*shakes her head*)

You don't seem to be doing very well with my questions. The **greenhouse effect** happens when the gas from burning coal and gasoline rises into my upper atmosphere. The gas absorbs ultraviolet radiation from the sun which warms the lower atmosphere. If my children continue to pollute my atmosphere, it will mean hotter summers and higher oceans. It will also harm all living things.

MOON

Let's hear it for Mother Earth!

MOTHER EARTH

Air pollution is not the only problem. **Water pollution** is becoming very harmful to my oceans, rivers, and lakes. How do my waters get polluted?

CLAIRE GLASS

It's the fishes' fault!

AL U. MINIUM

And it's the beavers' fault!

TIN TIN TIN

Bow wow, ruff, ruff, ruff, woof, ruff!

MOTHER EARTH (*annoyed*)

Absolutely not. My animals make their homes in or near my blue and green waters. They treat my waters kindly. No, it is not the fishes' and beavers' fault. And, Tin, you should not blame the frogs and the lobsters. Water pollution is caused by my other children, people, dumping chemicals and garbage into my lakes, rivers, and oceans. And ships have accidents and spill black, gooey oil.

MOON

Let's hear it for Mother Earth!

MOTHER EARTH (*shakes her head in disappointment*)

I don't know, panelists—we're not doing very well at all. Can anyone tell me what a **rainforest** is?

TIN TIN TIN

Woof, woof, woof, ruff, ruff.

MOTHER EARTH

Yes, Tin, in a way it is a forest where raindrops grow. **Rainforests** are large areas of my land where trees grow so close together, the leaves block out the sun. The water in the air rises, collects on the leaves, and falls back down as raindrops. The rainforests are important because they supply oxygen to my atmosphere.

MOON

Let's hear it for Mother Earth!

MOTHER EARTH

Can anybody tell me why I'm worried about my rainforests?

AL U. MINIUM AND CLAIRE GLASS

We didn't know you were worried.

MOTHER EARTH

Yes, I am worried. The rainforests are slowly being cut down and burned. Not only is my atmosphere being polluted with black smoke, but it is losing the precious oxygen it used to get from all those trees.

MOON

Let's hear it for Mother Earth!

MOTHER EARTH

As you know, my showers and rainstorms come from the evaporation of water from my lakes, rivers, and oceans. Can anybody tell me what **acid rain** is?

CLAIRE GLASS

Ask who about the rain?

AL U. MINIUM (*to Claire*)

She said ask Sid about the rain.

MOTHER EARTH

No, no. I didn't say "ask Sid." I said "acid." When certain chemicals rise into my atmosphere from burning gasoline (petrol) and coal, they change into acids. When the rain brings them back onto my surface, it is called acid rain. This acid slowly hurts my plants, animals, lakes, and trees.

MOON

Let's hear it for Mother Earth!

MOTHER EARTH

My last question is about my land. What is a **landfill**?

AL U. MINIUM
Is it the opposite of a landempty?

MOTHER EARTH (*encouraged*)
Now you're beginning to use your brains. A **landfill** is a place on my land where garbage and rubbish are buried. The problem is that these places are no longer empty. As a matter of fact, most of the landfills people have created are filled up. And there are very few empty ones left.

MOON
Let's hear it for Mother Earth!

TIN TIN TIN
Woof, ruff, ruff, bow wow.

MOTHER EARTH
Very good, Tin. This has led to **ocean dumping,** which is dumping garbage in the oceans. Does anyone know how you can solve the garbage problem?

AL U. MINIUM
By **recycling** aluminum cans.

CLAIRE GLASS
By **recycling** glass jars and bottles.

TIN TIN TIN
Ruff, *bow wow,* woof, woof.

MOTHER EARTH
Very, very good! **Recycling** aluminum and tin cans and glass containers is an important way to solve the landfill and ocean dumping problems. Metals and glass can be melted down and made into new cans, bottles, and jars. Not only does this save my sky, my land, and my deep blue seas, but it conserves my natural materials.

MOON
Let's hear it for Mother Earth!

MOTHER EARTH
It is now time to have a discussion. TV audience, the book *Cups & Cans & Paper Plate Fans* offers many ways to help me stay healthy. Do you have any other ideas or thoughts about what we talked about today?

(*The characters now have a discussion with the audience.*)

MOTHER EARTH
Now that we have exchanged ideas, I wish to thank everyone for taking part in today's important program. Remember, you only have one Mother Earth. Love me, respect me, and treat me kindly.

ALL
Good-bye!

(*After the bows, cover the screen with the poster board.*)

Index

Italics indicate illustration pages.